Bibliographic information published by the German National Library:

The German National Library lists this publication in the National Bibliography; detailed bibliographic data are available on the Internet at http://dnb.dnb.de .

Imprint:

Copyright © 2018 GRIN Verlag
Print and binding: Books on Demand GmbH, Norderstedt Germany
ISBN: 9783668901520

This book at GRIN:

https://www.grin.com/document/457830

Anonym

Behind the scenes of privacy. A quantitative research study to examine the influence of fear appeals on protection motivation

GRIN Verlag

GRIN - Your knowledge has value

Since its foundation in 1998, GRIN has specialized in publishing academic texts by students, college teachers and other academics as e-book and printed book. The website www.grin.com is an ideal platform for presenting term papers, final papers, scientific essays, dissertations and specialist books.

Visit us on the internet:

http://www.grin.com/

http://www.facebook.com/grincom

http://www.twitter.com/grin_com

Behind the scenes of privacy - a quantitative research study to examine the influence of fear appeals on protection motivation

Master's Thesis

Department of Information Systems and Services
University of Bamberg

Field of study: Internationale BWL
4. Semester

Abstract

This paper deals with the observable and recently emerging concerns of privacy online, such as possible information theft due to data leaks, and methods to motivate people conducting a more adequate behavior. The lack of existing academic literature and research on this phenomenon, is addressed by generating profound results regarding fear appeals and their impact on the intention for people to protect their data. An exploratory, quantitative study design is used, adopted from the protection motivation theory to primarily investigate the components of this model and the modifications of these by means of two groups, one experiencing fear appeals. A set of 25 questions was developed and surveyed within the scope of an online questionnaire. Analysis implied the existence of a positive relationship between fear appeals and protection intention valid. Furthermore, the results support the understanding of connections among the items prompted. The study contributes to the field of research by providing in-depth insights on the influence of fear appeals on the protection motivation. Based on these findings, the thesis concludes with theoretical as well as practical recommendations for future research.

Table of Contents

List of Figures

List of Tables

List of Abbreviations

BCG:	Boston Consulting Group
CA:	Cronbach's Alpha
DBIR:	Data Breach Investigations Report
GDPR:	European General Data Protection Regulation
EPPM:	Extended Parallel Process Model
IBM:	International Business Machines Corporation
ID:	Identification Number
InfoSec:	Information Security
IP:	Internet Protocol
IS:	Information Systems
ISec:	Information Security
IT:	Information Technology
NSA	National Security Agency
PMT:	Protection Motivation theory
PPM:	Parallel Process Model

List of Symbols

α: Cronbach's Alpha

β: Standardized Coefficient Beta

r^2:   R Square

r^2_{adj}:   Adjusted R Square

p: Coefficient Significance

1.   Introduction

Arguing that you don't care about the right to privacy because you have nothing to hide is no different than saying you don't care about free speech because you have nothing to say. - Edward Snowden (Romero 2015, p.2)

Due to the technological developments of the last 50 years, social networks - also called Web 2.0 technologies have a great influence on most people's lives. The internet is a platform for communication, information sharing and active participation in the design of media and virtual spaces in a society in which media is part of everyday life (Im and Baskerville 2005; McLoughlin and Lee 2007). The advantages of the global reach and pervasiveness of the internet for individuals are immense. Apart from facilitating normal everyday activities such as shopping, entertainment or information seeking, another advantage plays a major role: More than in any other time, the internet allows individuals to be more connected (Harrington et al. 2006). Not only single individuals benefit from the digitalization, also companies increasingly rely on technologies and the internet to survive and be successful in this competitive environment (Im and Baskerville 2005). As people leave more and more traces online, it became easier for companies to collect various data from users. Vast quantity of consumers information is needed in order for companies to sell better products directly tailored to the end users' needs (Culnan and Armstrong 1999).

As communication technology has evolved, so has the infringement of privacy online and various other security threats. Furthermore, the situation is a breeding ground for criminals and people with all kinds of malicious ambitions. They attempt to exploit end users who are not properly secured from online threats. These menaces include viruses, pishing, worms, trojan horses, spyware, malware and data breaches (Claar and Johnson 2012). Many known data breaches, which can be referred to as the unauthorized exposure of personal data through third parties, in recent years demonstrate the relevance of the issues (Cheng et al. 2017). A very significant incident with serious range has occurred on 8 on July this year with the company Timehop, an app that allows users to collect and be reminded of old photos and posts. Due to a data leak, 21 million accounts worldwide were compromised, 3.8 million users alone were affected in Europe. Among the data collected were 2.6 million genders, 2.9 million e-mail addresses, 2.6 million dates of birth and 243,000 phone numbers ("Timehop Data Breach: Millions of Users in Europe Compromised" 2018). Furthermore, the company IBM is the sponsor of the 13th annual Cost of a Data Breach study. Based on the study, which was carried out by the Ponemon Institute the average global cost of a data breach has increased to $3.86 million. This represents a growth rate of 6.4 % compared to the previous year. At the same time, the average expense of sensitive information stolen rose to 148 U.S. dollars. This represents an upturn of over 4.8 % ("Cost of Data Breach Study | IBM Security" 2018). Another incident of data leaks was initiated by internal staff gained immense public attention in June 2013, when Edward Snowden, the infamous whistleblower and former IT employee of the National Security Agency (NSA), handed over secret documents to the press. These documents revealed that the NSA was spying on the public while collecting personal information including public data, messages from different nationalities and even the communication systems of several governments around the world. This information could be collected by tapping their phone calls and e-mail services (Cole et al. 2015).

A not insignificant reason for data leaks and other security threats to happen is the negligent misconduct of individuals. Often, they are not aware of the seriousness of the situation and consequential do not consider protecting their data genuinely which makes their information easily accessible for others. In addition, they often do not take the security precautions necessary to be sufficiently protected against security threats (Posey et al. 2015). This negligence can indeed cause fatal consequences for individuals and companies. The repercussions of security threats are far-reaching: They can range from minor inconveniences to financial detriment and harm to the reputation of companies or theft damage to individuals (Harrington et al. 2006). When a company is the victim of such attacks, the data of the end users that the company has collected from them for various purposes is often under the control of a third party and far beyond the supervision of the company, not to mention out of the end users´ reach. The question now arises of whether a user would seek to improve their protection if they were aware of their lack of privacy online. The research question for this thesis therefore is:

Do people reconsider their behavior when they are informed that their data, such as passwords or e-mail addresses, are accessible by others on the internet?

The purpose of this paper is to analyze the privacy protection intention of end users online, by exposing them to fear appeals, persuasive messages emphasizing negative consequences of attitudes in order to motivate behavioral changes (Johnston and Warkentin 2010). These investigations performed are based on the protection motivation theory. This model is established on the assumption, that fear appeals result in people wanting to change behavior intentions (Gochman 1997). In the first instance, the paper sets out to provide an overview of the theoretical background of the terms privacy and the actual privacy concerns. The thesis is giving the reader a better understanding of information collection online as well as possible security threats occurring. A deeper insight of human errors in the process involved is provided and a review of the password behavior of end users is provided. After giving a short overview of fear appeals and different fear appeal models, the protection motivation theory and how it was applied in research so far is introduced. In the second part of the thesis, the research question is evaluated by conducting a quantitative study, which includes fear appeals trying to increase the individual's motivation for protecting their privacy online. Therefore, a survey participating 284 people was carried out. Gaining a deeper insight with analyzing, interpreting the results and presenting them to the reader, this paper offers various theoretical and practical implications for further research. The thesis concludes with a summary of the findings and ideas put forward.

.

2.   Theoretical Background

2.1   Privacy

Privacy is the claim of individuals, groups, or institutions to determine for themselves when, how, and to what extent information about them is communicated to others

– *Alan Westin* (Westin 1976,p.7)

As early as in 1967, Alan Westin described the functions of privacy in modern and dem-ocratic societies. He was, among other things, Professor of Public Law & Government Emeritus at the time. Westin divides private sphere into three different levels: privacy at political level, privacy at the socio-cultural and organizational level and the one at the individual level (Westin 1968). The latter, personal matters, being of major importance for this thesis. Privacy demands are made by every individual on a daily basis because the person strives for an inner-psychological balance between private sphere, commu-nication and the urge for disclosure. It should be remembered that in these dimensions the demands for an individual's personal space are continually varying. At a certain time, an individual wishes to have privacy and therefore to be left alone, at another time, the disclosure of private matters seems necessary for the very same individual. The ever-changing demands of individuals and decisions about self-disclosure make private space a question of personal choice. Westin therefore states that privacy is a funda-mental social property in democratic societies, and deserves support from the public. When asked in a survey, conducted by Harris-Westin in 2001, what the term means to individuals personally, intimacy was considered the most important closely followed by solitude, reserve and anonymity (Westin 2003). Those functions were published by Westin already in the year 1967. With terms of privacy, the individual is able to keep his true identity veiled. Even though one's actions can be observed by society, one can remain an unknown person. This gives an individual the freedom not to be dominated or manipulated by others. Westin states that individual's private sphere is an essential function for managing interpersonal communication. Every relationship is influenced, whether conscious or unconscious, by information individuals previously received about each other. Concluding, privacy allows individuals to distinguish between the content of transmitted information and the receptor of the provided information (Bradberry and Nemati 2014; Mai 2016). If an individual's information is released without their own con-sent, the right of free decision has been lost. Therefore, the term must be seen as a social good in democratic societies which requires constant support from the public (Regan 1995). These testimonies can be summed up by the statement Arthur Miller, political scientist, provided in 1971: *"The basic attribute of an effective right of privacy is the individual's ability to control the circulation of information relating to himself; a power that often is essential to maintaining social relationships and personal freedom."* (Miller and Zumbansen 2005).

In the context of information systems (IS) privacy is generally understood as the amount of supervision an individual has over their personal details (Bélanger and Crossler 2011). Current challenges in this context will be discussed in the next chapter.

2.2   Privacy Concerns – Actual Matters

On May 25, 2018, the new European General Data Protection Regulation (GDPR) entered into force. It unifies regulations for the processing of personal data. In the days following, the majority of Europeans received e-mails from companies and organizations which at some point they have given their contact details to or from which they regularly receive newsletters. Those concerned should then confirm that the contact or use of the data may continue. The new law replaces the 1995 EU Directive. Unlike the old one, the new regulation applies directly in all member states. This signifies that EU countries do not have to transpose the new rules into their own national law first. The aim is to harmonize data protection and better protect citizens in the digital age ("2018 Reform of EU Data Protection Rules" 2018). Due to those recent changes, personal data is under more protection, for example: name, address, e-mail address, ID number and IP address (European Commission 2018). More sensitive data about health or religious beliefs as well as the data of children are protected in particular, such information may only be processed in exceptional cases. In the case of children under the age of 16 years, parents must give their consent to the processing of data. In general, the following principles apply when dealing with personal data: Appropriation (data may only be used for a pre-defined, unambiguous, and legitimate purpose) Data minimization (declares that using personal data must be restricted to a defined and corresponding extent), Legitimacy and Transparence (data may only be used in a legitimate way which is understandable for the person in question), Limited storage duration (declares that data may only be stored as long as they are necessary for the purpose the data have been given for), Accuracy (all reasonable measures must be taken to ensure that inaccurate personal data is deleted or corrected immediately) and Integrity and Confidentiality (the adequate security of personal data, including protection against unauthorized or unlawful processing and against unintentional loss, destruction or damage ("Regulation (EU) 2016/679 of the European Parliament and of the Council of 27 April 2016" 2016). With the GDPR becoming applicable, companies will also be faced with a high administrative burden when it comes to any kind of security gaps, such as possible hacker attacks. However, the measures necessary to subsequently restore GDPR conformity can become much more problematic. Companies should therefore take a close look at their data system with regard to potential attack surfaces and check any back doors like backup devices ("Commission Staff Working Paper Impact Assessment /* SEC/2012/0072 Final */" 2018). The new policy portrays the importance of privacy and the associated data protection. Why this subject is so relevant will be explained in the following. In this section, a short overview on privacy concerns based on previous literature is provided.

As communication technology has evolved, so has the infringement of privacy (Pitta et al. 2003). In this growing environment, the user not only consumes the content, but also provides their own content as a prosumer (Liang and Xue 2010). On the personal level, sharing content via modern communication technologies, in many cases, is intended for close friends or targeted groups of people, but is often also accessible to remote acquaintances or even complete strangers. Many of these disclosures of personal information happen inadvertently and reach a wider audience than intended (Seligman and Csikszentmihalyi 2000). This comes from the circumstance that nowadays the internet is an environment in which it seems perfectly normal to disseminate sensitive data. The user voluntarily discloses private information such as addresses, dates of birth, activities, photos, locations, thoughts, feelings, experiences and preferences without a second thought and is indeed often encouraged to do so by the social environment.

Due to efficiency, exchange of information, reduced communication expenses, easy storage and retrieval of data the economy benefits greatly from communication technologies. They contribute a significant progress to businesses and can be seen as a single interdepend system (Alsunbul et al. 2016). Companies strive to build their own sustainable market positions with the aid of digitalization (Alqahtani et al. 2014). One of the main components of mass customization nowadays is in-depth knowledge of the end users characteristics as well as their diverse and unique preferences. This allows the supplier to provide highly specific and satisfying products and services to the individual customer (Habryn and Kunze 2012). Whilst the use of potential customers' information is beneficial for various companies, one has to be aware of its extent of dissemination of personal data online. The following examples give an insight of how easily personal data is made available on the internet. In addition to all the advantages for companies and the economy, one consequence is that companies have processed and stored most of the personal data digitally. First, Electronic health records show a lack of security. They acquire data on patients which contains information about all physical and mental illnesses in digital form. Also, the processing of health-related claims due to insurance reasons demands the exchange of health records. However, this information is provided to anyone who is able to access it, which makes the data available to others in an unidentified, aggregated way and not only to the medical professionals affected. The personal information is now out of control of the local health care provider and has been passed on to some, for the individual unknown, remote bureaucrats (Angst and Agarwal 2009). Second, money and credit matters require an exchange of data between credit institutions, debts and loans also included in this information. The emergence of national electronic transactions, often through the use of credit cards, has exacerbated this. National databases with consumer's financial data are generated and, as a result, individuals are no longer in full control over their data (Pitta et al. 2003).

These developments and trends have challenged end users to face new emerging types of privacy issues and information security: With the increasing development and importance of technology, the definition of privacy has been expanded. Data protection, also often referred to as information security (ISec or InfoSec), is one of these, a subgroup of general privacy (Phelps et al. 2000). Data protection is a multi-faceted, very complex and context-specific construct. Legal and regulatory frameworks, cultural standards and security mechanisms affect data protection (Galanxhi and Nah 2006). Nowadays, protecting online data has become a challenging subject in society. This is mainly the situation for younger people, due them having different viewpoints on security online and the associated practices (Yoon et al. 2012). Protection of data indicates that personally identifiable information is unavailable to other people or organizations in general. In case of this data becoming available to any other party nevertheless, the person affected must be in a position to have a significant degree of control over the information and its usage (Westin 2003). Summarizing, privacy is an individual's decision to manage communication, on which personal information should be externalized and which should be kept private. Therefore, data protection is the ability of people to monitor the gathering and processing of their personal data (Mai et al. 2010). The willingness to protect data also depends on how sensitive the information is. Most people do not care if someone knows their first name, thus users are willing to divulge this information, as for them personally it is insensitive data. In contrast, one very rarely willingly discloses sensitive data such as their own body weight or sexual experiences (Grossklags and Acquisti 2007).

End users are indeed attaching increasing importance to their privacy and are seeking to protect it. Users are required to maintain a healthy balance between the correct level of disclosure and retention of personal information online. End users, whether inside an organization or within the environment of home computing, have critical assets that require to be protected from various levels of security breaches and data theft (Menard et al. 2017). Partly, privacy has become a shield. If a consumer is confronted with too many requests for information, their privacy becomes an excuse. In response to this question, some now reject all communication. A survey by AT Kearny showed that 52% of the interviewees decide to discontinue an online purchasing transaction for data protection reasons (Ranganathan 2002). It has also been stated that 30-40% of customers enter false information online. This is due to the desire for anonymity, as well as the ability to avoid spam e-mails and the uncertainty as to how the website deals with personal data (Van Dyke et al. 2007). Metzger and Doctor have reviewed opinion surveys on online privacy in 2003 between 1998 and 2001. It emerged that 74% of respondents were concerned about their privacy on the internet (Yao et al. 2007). In his paper, Kshetri gives an overview of surveys conducted with both companies and customers. They proof that companies as well as individuals are concerned about their privacy. A survey was conducted earlier this year by the research and consulting company Ovum, sponsored by data security business Vormetric. The sample consisted of 500 decision-makers from medium and large IT companies in Germany, Great Britain and France. The results show that 53% of the respondents were concerned about lack of security in the online environment. In the same year, a SAP study that included 300 mobile operators found that 38% of the respondents said privacy and security issues were preventing companies from realizing their full potential. The results of the consumer surveys showed similar results. In 2013 BCG conducted a survey of 10.000 consumers from 12 countries. The results show that 75% of the respondents replied that data protection is a "top issue" for them. Only 7% would be comfortable with their data being used for anything other than the original purpose. Ovum also found similar results in the same year. 11,000 people from over 11 different countries were included in the surveys. 68% would use a "do not track function" if it was easily available in a search engine. Moreover, only 14% believed that companies were honest about the use of personal data (Kshetri 2014).

In regard of these current developments, the growing tendency to protect consumers right to privacy is a major obstacle and conflict to the acquisition of this knowledge (Alashoor et al. n.d.). In order to understand the concerns of privacy, the next section provides some background information on the collection of data online to the reader.

2.3   Collection of Information – General Overview

In the past, the owner of the corner shop, the family doctor and maybe the barkeeper in the local pub knew about the preferences of individuals, knew their needs, their disposable budget, as well as family secrets. Such relationships were based on face-to-face communication. As conducted above, the reality nowadays looks different due to exten-sive data collection and storage online. Two reasons can be attributed to this phenom-enon: First, businesses rely on vast volumes of knowledge to develop stronger relation-ships with current clients and acquire new ones. Second, as mentioned above, infor-mation technology is enhancing productivity and reducing costs. As a result, information can now be used in ways that once were either impractical or economically inconvenient (Culnan and Armstrong 1999). For companies, the ownership of end user data is be-coming increasingly important. To survive and succeed, companies depend on a large amount of personalized information. The more extensive the data, the greater and more influential the reach. This serves to strengthen existing customer relationships and to win new customers (Awad and Krishnan 2006).

On the one hand, benefits of using the collected data correctly include among others higher quality products, elaborate customer service and customized products that meet the customers' needs. This brings advantages for the company as well as the customer. On the other hand, a significant disadvantages is the invasion of the customers' privacy. There is a growing tension between gathering and utilizing of individual data, which is disclosed in the plurality of online operations and the private sphere. Therefore, the same practices that are beneficial to companies also raise concerns about privacy for people (Culnan and Armstrong 1999; Van Dyke et al. 2007). To get an exact overview of how data collection functions two major categories of data usage have to be distin-guished: the primary and secondary use. The first utilization of gathered personal infor-mation can be determined as an organization's application of the data to create con-sumer profiles and therefore enhance sales and customer services. In this case, cus-tomers are willing to reveal personal data (Culnan 1993). In contrast to the primary use, where the allocation of data happens with authorization from the individuals, secondary use of data includes the disclosure of personal data to third parties who were not part of the initial operation. When information is collected from users for one particular rea-son, but is used for a different purpose without the permission or even the user's aware-ness, it is referred to as secondary use of data (Smith et al. 1996). Concluding the same information will be used for a purpose other than the original intent of the acquisition. If more and more parties can now access the personal data of individuals, the various security threats have a broader reach. These endangerments will be discussed in more detail in the next chapter.

2.4   Security Threats and Human Errors

Information on a sheet of paper is always visible and users have the advantage of being able to control their data or, if necessary, destroy it forever, e.g. by shredders. Online, the individuals control is much more limited. As more and more households use the internet and broadband, consumers face new sources of danger (Pitta et al. 2003).

With the development of such an interdependent environment and the significant online presence of the user, it is becoming a lot easier for hackers to gain access to an indi-viduals' computer. This may result in simple inconveniences e.g. erasure of important, private files. But online security threats can appear in many forms and some scenarios are far less appealing (Harrington et al. 2006). Social engineering attacks like phishing aim at getting users to disclose sensitive data. Malware results in infections such as computer viruses, which are supposed to cause damage. Trojan horses are created to provide to transmit a virus or a spyware, or computer worms that are able to propagate as rapidly and disrupt the network. This kind of malware interferes with the general operation of an infected computer and is quite noticeable for the user. However, a more common type of malware is imperceptibly located on the host computers and attempts to steal private or online activity data stored on the computer (Claar and Johnson 2012). Furthermore, social networking sites are often used by hackers to infect individuals' computers with malware like viruses or worms. A frequent scenario includes Facebook members sharing a YouTube-link with a group of friends. In order to display the enclosed video, one is required to download an "update" of some sort. By updating, users download malware that is infecting the computer with so-called "bots" that allow hackers to use the computers whenever and however they want and therefore join a bigger "botnet" (Crossler and Bélanger 2014). Bots are versatile as they let the hacker running the malware control administrative privileges on the affected person's computer completely. Then, the hacker is able to use the computer to execute distributed denial-of-service attacks on different servers, spread spam, open backdoors on the personal computer or install software to detect keystrokes, the efficiency of a software, on the computer of the person affected. A study by MacAfee Avert Labs reports that over 12 million new machines were integrated into botnets worldwide in the first quarter of 2009 (Claar and Johnson 2012). The consequences of a hacker attack with malware eventually lead to financial harm and damage of reputation for businesses or theft losses for individuals. In addition, these attacks are increasingly targeting private parties, resulting in significant financial burdens for them. Furthermore, the effectiveness of the internet's infrastructure is affected (Harrington et al. 2006). Since home computers can be made part of botnets very quickly and easily, this evolves in a considerable number of problems for private users, companies and governments.

Another topical security threat that has recently been highlighted by various public incidents are data breaches. A data breach can be defined as an occurrence that results in a confirmed disclosure of sensitive personal data to unauthorized third parties. These incidents are often carried out by hackers or other parties that have no entitlement to access this information. This term is a generic term for data leaks, which can be described as the deliberate or accidental disclosure of sensitive personal data. The origins could be based on internal processes or errors. Both lead to consumer data being publicly exposed in some way. These exposures not only represent a major threat to companies but can also have serious consequences for individuals. Furthermore, the loss of sensitive information can gravely damage a company's reputation. Financial losses or even the long-term survival of the company can also be at stake. The information can range from customer data on intellectual property to published medical records. Data leakage can occur in two ways: internal or external information breaches. They can happen either intentionally or accidentally. The first would be data theft by invaders or sabotage by offenders. The latter can be understood as the inadvertent disclosure of sensitive data by employees and associates. The procedure for the first type is as follows: The attacker is looking for ways to get into the target system. For vulnerabilities found in the area of infrastructure, targeted attacks in the form of, for example, attempts to deceive with the help of phishing or spam. As soon as access is obtained in step two, the data is actually stolen by the attacker transferring the data from the target system. (Cheng et al. 2017; Web Application Security Consortium: Threat Classification 2004)

A study by Intel Security5 has revealed that the internal staff is responsible for 43% of data leaks. Furthermore, 43% of data leaks are random. Among other things, industrial espionage or financial threats etc. can be regarded as motivations for this. The unintended incidents, are often due to inadequate business workflows. This includes, for example, the non-application of preventive technologies or security guidelines. In 2013, credit and debit card information of about 40 million customers of Target Corporation had been stolen and other information for 70 million people, including e-mail and mailing addresses, had also been exposed. To date, customers have suffered financial losses of $248 million. A year later, about 500 million accounts were stolen in an apparent "state-sponsored" data breach of Yahoo (Cheng et al. 2017).

Another 25 percent of recorded safety violations are caused by end users (Mylonas et al. 2013). This is due to the fact that people cannot be supervised by technical solutions (Siponen and Oinas-Kukkonen 2007). Inside the organizational context, employees are usually the most vulnerable component of information security (Bulgurcu et al. 2010; Im and Baskerville 2005). Many companies state their staff can be considered the weakest link in protecting organizational assets. At the same time, co-workers could make a major contribution to reducing the risks when applying adequate protective behavior (Bulgurcu et al. 2010). This statement will be addressed in more detail below. Therefore, it is important that companies protect the systems with the information they contain, as they increasingly rely on it for transmission, processing and storage (Ng et al. 2009). Thus it is not surprising that compliance with security guidelines by employees have evolved into an important socio-organizational asset (Bulgurcu et al. 2010). Summarizing, behavior of individuals may have far-reaching consequences that cross borders between people, organizations and nations. As a consequence, the demand of promoting appropriate individual safety behavior both at work and at home is higher than ever (Harrington et al. 2006). The deployment of Anti-Virus software, anti-spyware software, identity theft prevention services and automated cloud-based backup solutions are only a few examples of effective resources that home users are investing for protection of their personal assets (Menard et al. 2017). Although, this being a step in the right direction, it is hard for users to keep this precautious behavior on a routine level. Despite using those various protection services, home users tend to stick with poor passwords, share passwords with others in order to co-use streaming accounts like Netflix, to open unknown links or to override security warnings whilst installing applications (Menard et al. 2017) . Even when security behavior has been studied on mobile devices, the search results show that the current security warnings of an app repository tend to become ineffective over time, as users are likely to click through them. It was also found that people tend to overlook the reputation and ratings of an application as well as safety and agreement messages that were detected from App repositories during application installation (Mylonas et al. 2013).

The risks and negative scenarios mentioned above could be largely reduced or eliminated if home users changed their passwords regularly, used stronger key words, kept their anti-virus software up to date, set up firewalls and exercised caution when opening e-mails and attachments or other links sent to them on social media platforms. Nevertheless, some studies show that there is a large disparity between the awareness of the individual in relation to their safety and the manifestations of security threats in reality. These characteristics apply not only to home users but also to employees of various companies (Harrington et al. 2006) For example, another study by America Online and the National Cyber Security Alliance with 329 participants showed that approximately 75% of the participants believe their system is much protected against online assaults and viruses. For this reason, 84% of the participants hold confidential data on their computer and 72% make sensible transfers on their PC. A review of the systems of the interviewees revealed that 15% had no antivirus software in use (Claar and Johnson 2012). At the workplace, guidelines containing regulations on essential safety behavior can be created. In addition, training courses can be held and behavior can be monitored. Furthermore, sanctions may be imposed to ensure compliance with such safety practices (Harrington et al. 2006). While, as already mentioned above, organizations make great efforts to ensure information security, this cannot be accomplished by using technological tools alone. Inquiries into what has caused the latest security breaches have revealed that the negligence of employees has led to infringements costing companies millions. Many breaches were caused by carelessness or ignorance of security policies by employees (Herath et al. 2012). These measures only apply to companies and home users who are often left alone with only their own responsibility or discipline to indulge in such security activities.

In summary, the great majority of online users indeed understands how to apply protection methods but still often neglects to take them, even though they mostly acknowledge themselves as the ones to be accountable for their security behavior rather than the government or software companies (Claar and Johnson 2012).

2.5   Password Behavior of End Users

User names and passwords have been the preferred method of user authentication for many decades due to their low cost of implementation (Herley and Van Oorschot 2012). Entering a password is the predominant method to ensure personal assets, such as personal e-mails, financial information, and privacy of end users online. Among the primary objectives of code word usage is the prevention of hacker attacks (Zhang and McDowell 2009). Nevertheless, there are some problems and challenges associated with the use of passwords for many end users, as difficulties with the performance of key word compliance can appear (Mwagwabi et al. 2018a). Experts confirm the problems resulting from the reckless usage of passwords by stating that code words are among the most common risk elements for human errors (Carstens et al. 2004). The effects of poor password management habits are tangible. In 2009 for example, an unauthorized party hacked into a Twitter corporate account. He managed to gain access to the employee's personal e-mail account and other sensitive data as they were not adequately protected due to poor code word practice and failure to comply with password policies. This case is one of many examples, that non-complex passwords can have an enormous impact not only on the personal level, but also on the organizational level (Mwagwabi et al. 2018a). Moreover, a study which investigated the security of online passwords found that out of 516 end user accounts examined, almost a third could be breached within a minute. The other accounts were bursted open within four hours (Zhang and McDowell 2009). Another showcase of the severity associated with password management is the Verizon Data Breach Investigations Report (DBIR) from the year 2015. It provides an overview of the extent to which legitimate user data (login IDs and code words) was used in 2015, accounting for 50% of all reported data breaches. After an evaluation of 2260 confirmed data breaches, 63% of the tested accounts use Not only are those figures presented above alarming, they also raise the question of how a poor password is defined.

According to Zhang and McDowell, a strong password is a code word consisting of at least 12 alphanumeric characters, upper and lower-case letters, a minimum of one number and at least one special character. Examples of weak code words include words like "password" or numerical orders like "123456" or contain significant personal information. They are used on an alarming rate by end users, even when sensitive data such as financial accounts are involved (Florencio and Herley 2007; Zhang and McDowell 2009). In addition, due to the number of websites individuals are registered on, many end users pick the same codes for various websites. When more complex passwords are being created, owners tend note their complicated combination of letters and numbers somewhere. This again leads to a security gap (Das et al. 2014). Even the application of a very strong keyword to more than one account is hazardous, as only one account has to be compromised for having negative effects on all the other accounts (Stephen 2016). One momentous issue, where the correct application of strong passwords would be of importance are e-mails. Almost all web users access e-mails on a daily basis. However, they are an easy target for a series of security threats. Mails are frequently misused to gain access to personal and financial records through phishing and spamming, exposing users to theft of identity and online fraud (Herath et al. 2012). This can be attributed to the fact that people are often registered with the same e-mail addresses on most social media platforms.

Due to this current situation, there are several website manufacturers and various companies that offer information for users on how to generate more powerful passwords. For example, the company Google provides tips for generating a safe password as well as a password strength meter. The latter evaluates the passwords according to their strength. This is determined from the length of the password and the composition of the characters. Furthermore, weak options such as the word "password" are getting declined. Those weak passwords may not be used on the website (Zhang and W. McDowell 2009). Microsoft also takes its safety measures: In order to create an account, a mixture of letters and numbers and a minimum keyword length is required. These are particularly useful for the end user at home, as they do not benefit from integrated network applications that are available for most of the employees at their workplace. The latter often require a special type of password procedure. Another way to encourage users to create stronger passwords are special password management applications which save all keywords in a cryptographically secured place which is then only accessible through an ideally strong master password phrase, thereby decreasing the workload of storing many unique and strong passwords (Huth et al. 2012).

However, a study shows that despite existing rules on how users should compose their passwords, these are often not adhered to. Many attempts trying to lead end users to the usage of stronger passwords do not have the desired effect. Visual guides, such as code word strength meters on websites, do not motivate end users to use stronger codes. It is evident that many end users still tend to choose weak ones instead (Vance et al. 2013). There are several approaches to explain this phenomenon. One reason for users still preferring simple passwords may be that, as password policies differ from page to page, end users find it difficult to remember the various different passwords.

This in turn has a negative effect on the security of the specific page concerned (Beautement et al. 2008; Bonneau and Preibusch 2010). The same holds true for guide-lines on pages that demand a monthly keyword reset. Due to the amount of overhead this causes, users are easily tempted to choose passwords that are easy to guess (Adams and Sasse 1999). A further approach, and probably the most common reason, is that most end users still find it difficult to remember complex code words and therefore use the ones common to them (Ur et al. 2012).

2.6   Fear Appeals

Fear appeals are persuasive messages designed to scare people by describing the terrible things that will happen to them if they do not do what the message recom-mends.

- Kim Witte (Johnston and Warkentin 2010, p.551)

In order to motivate individuals to behave in an adaptive way, fear appeals have been used for many years in convincing messages. These are not only used in research of information security, but derive much more from the research of the field of health awareness and health communication (Roskos-Ewoldsen et al. 2004). They are per-suasive messages designed to alarm people of potential threats by declaring the terri-fying consequences of not acting in accordance with the message. The main goal of fear appeals is to create transformation through persuasiveness (Johnston and Warkentin 2010; Mwagwabi et al. 2018b). The importance of fear in fear arousing com-munication was already known as early as in 1992 when Witte published her work "Put-ting the fear back into fear appeals" in the same year (Han n.d.).The necessary ele-ments of a fear appeal include the individual susceptibility to threats, assessments of the severity of threats, efficacy in terms of a suggested reaction and the individual's capacity to respond as recommended. A correctly designed fear appeal not only serves to provide information about the existence of a threat, but also to communicate the se-verity of the danger and the vulnerability of the affected target. Concluding, the main components of a fear appeal are: fear, threat and effectiveness (Johnston and Warkentin 2010; Witte 1992).

A threat can be described as an extrinsic stimulus. This is irrespective of whether the treat is perceptible by a person or not. If an individual is perceiving a threat, the person has an adequate understanding of it. From this message, it is possible for an individual to express the perceived threat severity and the perceived threat susceptibility (Johnston and Warkentin 2010; Witte 1992). The first one can be described as a per-son's beliefs about the gravity of an existing threat whereas the perceived vulnerability expresses a person's conviction of the chances that this threat will occur (Witte 1992). Fear appeals often take the form of notices or messages, and serve as a mechanism for manipulation and are geared to the execution of a corresponding protective behavior (Johnston and Siponen 2015). Furthermore, they usually provide practicable sugges-tions that are described as being powerful in countering the threat (Johnston et al. 2015). Witte suggests that a fear arousing communication contains two parts: state-ments designed to raise the perceived threat and the effort to increase the perceived effectiveness in the framework of a suggested reaction (Witte 1994). The former is achieved by highlighting the severity of the threat (i.e. the level of damage related to the threat) and the likelihood of the threat appearing. The latter emphasizes the clear and practicable measures to avert the threat and the importance of the suggested response to do so (Johnston and Warkentin 2010; Witte 1994). If an appeal of fear leads to a significant threat perception, an assessment follows of the response effectiveness and the ability to immediately implement the response (self-efficacy). In circumstances when the perceived threat is associated with a modest to high degree of perceived efficacy, an individual will adopt measures to reduce the threat (Johnston and Siponen 2015). The capability to perform the suggested action is critical. This improves self-efficacy, which will be defined in the following chapter. For this reason, the appeals of fear provide guidance on how to follow the recommended procedure (Woon et al. 2015). Furthermore, a fear arousing communication is therefore an incentive to stimulate fear as well as threat and coping assessment processes. In the ideal case, a fear appeal would not only increase the threat, but would also enhance the effectiveness by giving a respondent a way to tackle the threat. It is important that qualified fear appeals generate both high levels of threat and effectiveness, as they appeal to the threat as well as the capacity of the individual to respond (Boss et al. 2015). Concluding, according to this it is not only essential that a fear appeal is used to trigger fear, but also to use it to the right extent in order to have the right consciousness to this extent. It is therefore important that the person concerned develops the awareness for the danger, only then they will act accordingly.

2.7   Development of Fear Appeal Theories and Models

For decades scientists and psychologists have been researching why individuals react positively to some messages contained in fear appeals, whereas others do not show any response at all. Various different theories and models have been developed and applied in the research of fear appeals and information security (Boss et al. 2015; Johnston and Warkentin 2010).

Information Security, abbreviated as ISec or InfoSec, can be seen as the technical part of privacy. According to the international standard, ISec refers to the maintenance of integrity, non-disclosure and the accessibility of information and data (von Solms and van Niekerk 2013). This definition applies to the personal dimension as well as on the organizational level (Awad and Krishnan 2006). Furthermore, the term describes a process, and is not to be confused with a technology or a product. The primary objective is to guarantee the continuance of organizations as well as the reduction of damages within the businesses. Information security achieves these goals by minimizing the consequences of security incidents and to secure absence of security gaps (von Solms and van Niekerk 2013). To achieve this state, a multi-faceted collaboration of technical and organizational topics and events in the external context is essential (Dutta and Roy n.d.). Nowadays, research commonly uses the protection motivation theory to support the investigations (Boss et al. 2015; Johnston and Warkentin 2010). In order to understand the development and the usage of this theory in research, one has to gain a basic understanding of its origin. The following section presents three basic models to provide insights of the underlying assumptions and constraints of the protection motivation theory. The models presented below are, according to scientists, the basis in the field of fear appeal research and in the field of ISec. The following theories were each developed in the 1950s and 1970s and aim to investigate the individual's response to fear appeals. Hence, they were being used by the majority of scientists in this time period (Johnston and Warkentin 2010; Roskos-Ewoldsen et al. 2004). The models presented are the following: fear-as-acquired drive model, and the parallel process model with a look at its extended version, the extended parallel process model.

The fear as acquired drive model, also known as drive reduction model, was first implemented by Hovland et al. in 1953 and therefore counts as one of the earliest approaches to address the motivation of individuals for the adoption of persuasive messages. This pioneering theory was modified by Janis in 1967. It regards the persuasive effect of appeals of fear as an emotional process. The emotion fear is hereby considered as a drive, whereby it is understood as an unpleasant feeling of inner tension and restlessness, which should lead the individuals to perform a desired behaviorr (de Hoog et al. 2008). The correlation between fear and motivation can be seen as an inverse U-shaped correlation. According to Janis, there must be a certain amount of fear to motivate behavior that is consistent with mitigating the threat. But, in contrast, excessive fear could lead to behavior that is compatible with the alleviation of the threat (Johnston and Warkentin 2010). In this case, the person will find alternative approaches to overcome fear (Boss et al. 2015). Therefore, Janis states, that the negative emotional state generated drives individuals to take actions that decrease their personal fear (Johnston and Warkentin 2010). Concluding, this model implies that greater concern would therefore result in more persuasiveness, but only when the proposed action is considered as being effective for security purposes (de Hoog et al. 2008). McGuire also stated in 1968/1969 that supports Janis' assumption by also outlining an inverse U-shaped relationship between the existence of fear and behavioral change. McGuire declared when fear served as a drive, individuals followed procedures that were in accordance with the suggested actions of this message. In contrast, when fear was the cue, the desired recommendations for action were not made because accustomed responses to fear prevented the recommended actions (Johnston and Warkentin 2010). However, due to science and research of these the two above-mentioned statements by Janis and McGuire, their models since have been strongly rejected because no evidence of proof has been found to support these theories. The main reason is that, in the end, it was never possible to support a direct relationship between drive and behavioral adaption (Leventhal 1970; Witte 1992).

In 1970, Leventhal developed the parallel process model, also referred to as PPM. Based on the assumptions of the fear-as-acquired drive model, the psychologist expanded the concept of duality of answers and developed his model to differentiate between two different reactions that occur in fear: the primary cognitive process and the primary emotional process. The former, the danger prevention process, leads to reflections about the risks and consequently actions are carried out to avoid them. The latter is a process of controlling fear. This leads people to have their anxiousness under control through avoidance, ignorance, etc. However, the reasons for the development of individual processes when they occur are lacking in this model. About 22 years later, in 1992, there was an extended version published: the extended parallel process model, short EPPM. This extended model, which also contains elements from the PMT presented below, specifies some derivations of the two responses to fear appeals (Popova 2012; Witte 1992). In the view of the EPPM, the evaluation of a fear arousing communication triggers two evaluative measures of the message that result either in a mastery of danger control processes or fear control processes (Witte 1992). Therefore, in sum-mary, the extended parallel process model is able to declare as to when and why fear is effective or when it fails. The EPPM and, just like its most closely related model the protection motivation theory, have many strengths that make these models very attrac-tive for scientists and their research (Popova 2012).

The next section gives a detailed overview of the protection motivation theory men-tioned above and explains why this model was chosen as the basis for the following research study conducted in order to answer the research question in this thesis.

2.8   Protection Motivation Theory

A minimum level of threat or concern must exist before people start contemplating the benefits of possible actions and ruminate their competence to actually perform them.

                        – Ralf Schwarzer   (Gochman 1997, p.113)

This quote by Schwarzer, already made in 1992, sums up the core statement behind the protection motivation theory hereafter abbreviated with PMT. The model was first developed by Rogers in 1975 and investigates which variables are involved in control-ling health related behavior (Gochman 1997). PMT was developed using determinants from previous theories, in particular in the parallel process model presented in the pre-vious section (Ifinedo 2012; Ranganathan and Grandon 2002). It was originally devel-oped in the field of health care and is derived from personal threats, directed straight against an individual. The core idea behind this theory is the motivation behind the de-fense resulting from a perceptual threat and the willingness to eliminate a potential neg-ative outcome (Menard et al. 2017).

It is one of the "fear appeal theories" and originally examines the impact of endangering health warnings on changes on mindsets and behavior of individuals (Lee et al. 2008; Lee 2011). As the perception of danger and the motivational role of threats plays an important role, it is assumed to inspire people to move towards healthy and protective action. Concluding, the model is based on the assumption that fear, such as experi-enced health threats, lead to people wanting to change their health behavior, more pre-cisely, they want to change the intentions of their health behavior. Examples of those health threats according to Rogers and Prentice-Dunn could include: unhealthy diet, little exercise, abuse of tobacco and alcohol and other potentially risky habits, which they refer to as "lifestyle illnesses" (Gochman 1997). Beyond the health care sector, PMT is also suitable for the environment of ISec where users, employees and custom-ers require an additional level of motivation to secure their information assets. The com-puter does not only serve as a source of entertainment, it is also heavily integrated into the everyday life and reaches the position of an extension of the self. Thus, one can simply find strong parallels to personal health behavior and the health of your own com-puter reaches the same great importance (Lee et al. 2008). Just like an unhealthy body, an unhealthy computer has a negative impact on one's everyday life. The theory was adapted and applied by many ISec researchers. It is used to explain the individual's tendency to voluntary, safe behavior (Boss et al. 2015; Menard et al. 2017). One reason for its application in this field of research is that the model is able to explain the security behavior of individuals outside a corporate context and thus elucidates why people take certain countermeasures to protect and prevent computer threats (Crossler 2010).The protection motivation theory is inferior to some changes over time. In the first version, the "core nomology", the factor fear has been recognized, but not yet integrated. In a later version, the "full nomology" the variable fear and the maladaptive rewards were integrated and are part of the model. In this thesis, that version is used in the research model because fear is an important component in the quantitative study which will be explained in more detail in a later section (Boss et al. 2015).

In the following sections, there will be a short overview of the revised version of the PMT model. The usage of the model will be explained, the individual components illustrated in detail and the fear appeal discussed.

2.8.1 Design of the Protection Motivation Theory

In summary, PMT describes the procedure that initiates the receiving of information (information sources), which causes the person to evaluate the given content (cognitive mediating process) and to ultimately use the information and take action (coping mode) (Crossler and Bélanger 2014).

In more detail, the sources of information can be divided into environmental ones as well as intrapersonal ones. The cognitive mediation process is furthermore divided into two big dimensions which both influence the protection motivation of an individual, the intention to fulfill recommended behavior of limiting future risks. The two dimensions influencing the protection motivation are: the treat appraisal and the coping appraisal. The threat appraisal contains three variables: the perceived severity of a threatening event, the perceived vulnerability and maladaptive rewards. Response-efficacy, self-efficacy as well as response costs outline the coping appraisal. The coping mode consists of adaptive coping as well as maladaptive coping (Gochman 1997). A self-determined, overall view of the protection motivation theory model, adapted from Rogers and Prentice-Dunn, is provided in Figure 1. Figure 2 shows the cognitive mediating process of the PMT. Both will be explained in more detail in the following sections.

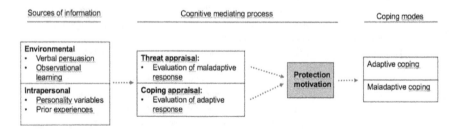

Figure 1: Overall Model of the PMT, own Representation based on Rogers and Prentice-Dunn (Gochman 1997)

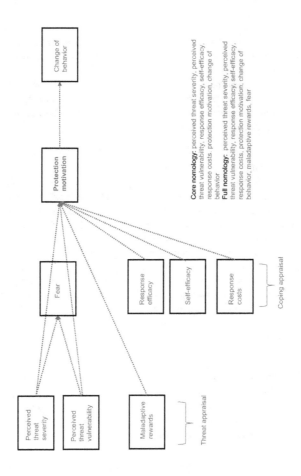

Figure 1: Cognitive Mediating Process of PMT, own representation based on Boss et al (Boss et al. 2015).

2.8.2 Sources of Information

Sources of information may be divided into two categories: environmental information and intrapersonal information.

Environmental information are sources of information which can include conversations with or instructions from other people such as family members, friends, acquaintances in reality as well as on social media etc. about threats and possible protective responses (verbal persuasion). Environmental information sources can also be direct witnesses of victimization actions or the use of protective responses (observational learning) – seeing what happens to others (Crossler and Bélanger 2014; Crossler 2010). In his model, Rogers differentiates between two intrapersonal sources of information: personality variables and prior experiences. Intrapersonal sources of information refer to the individuals' personality, the characteristics or former experiences of the individual. Those can influence their perception of the threat or their willingness to take protective action (Gochman 1997).

2.8.3 Cognitive Mediating Process

Considering the PMT model, one has to distinguish between the evaluation of maladaptive response (threat appraisal), fear, the assessment of the adaptive response (coping appraisal) and their influence on the intention to perform protective behavior optimally leading to change of behavior. Studies in other IS security fields demonstrate an expansion of PMT to cover a connection made between intentions and actual behavior (LaRose et al. 2008; Liang and Xue 2010). Regarding the health care context, for most health issues, there may be only one maladaptive and one adaptive response. An example from the health sector is smoking – two possibilities: either one is smoking or one stops smoking. For the remaining amount of health problems, there may be more than one response. For example can more than one reason be the response for being unhealthy. Probably there is an improper diet or the individual is not exercising enough (Gochman 1997).

2.8.3.1 Threat Appraisal

The affected person assesses in the process of maladaptive response, the potential advantages of starting or maintaining the current lifestyle, even though this exposes him to possible negative consequences. Therefore, it can be said that threat assessment is a factor impacting whether a person accepts a particular coping response (Crossler et al. 2014).

The threat appraisal characteristics that enhance the probability of maladaptive reaction are intrinsic and extrinsic rewards. Intrinsic rewards can be seen as physical pleasure while performing a specific activity. A person is extrinsically motivated when external incentives such as remuneration or recognition from a third party etc. play a decisive role in the individuals actions. This can be peer groups or social media. Extrinsic and intrinsic rewards can be summarized as maladaptive rewards and are therefore referred to with this term in the following. While these two factors can encourage a person to engage in behaviors that may expose them to potential threats, there are two other factors that reduce the possibility of maladaptive behavior (Gochman 1997). These two factors are perceived threat severity and perceived threat vulnerability. Perceived severity can be seen as the degree of consequences, like physical and psychological harm (e.g. effect on self-esteem) or social threats on family or friends that result from a threatening event. Furthermore, perceived severity has a positive impact on the individuals protection motivation (Crossler and Bélanger 2014). ISec research confirms this statement by saying that if one perceives the severity of a threat, it increases the probability that people will adhere to the proposed recommendations for action. In their research, Woon et al. ascertained that users tend to enable wireless security measures when they believe that a breach of their wireless home network would be harmful. It is now possible to establish a direct relationship between perceived severity and protection motivation where the likelihood of individuals complying with security policies is greatest if they believe that the threats would be harmful to them or their organization. Concluding, people will take to heart password security recommendations if they feel that the consequences of a data leak can be serious (Mwagwabi et al. 2018b; Woon et al. 2015).

Perceived vulnerability can be defined as the estimation of an individual's exposure to the threat, the likelihood of an impending security event occurring. Furthermore it is assumed to have a positive correlation with protection motivation intentions. An example from ISec research is the password security of the individual, since passwords can often be guessed by hackers or even be assessed by a program. This program ascertains passwords by searching for possible combinations which are often used in passwords combinations (Crossler and Bélanger 2014; Zhang and McDowell 2009).

2.8.3.2 Fear

The factor fear, influences the assessment of the severity of danger and therefore indirectly behavior and change in behavior. Fear can have an indirect and detrimental effect on the change of attitude by causing inappropriate management, in particular the avoidance of defensive measures (Gochman 1997). Fear was already noticed in the penultimate version of the PMT, but only in the last version, the complete PMT model, it was explained as an important dimension. Research often does not integrate the component of fear in research or does not measure its, leading to mixed results in the studies. Therefore, there is a need to gain a better understanding of the importance of this variable and its implementation in research (Boss et al. 2015; Zhang et al. 2009).

2.8.3.3 Coping Appraisal

In the process of the adaptive response, the individual assesses the capacity for risk prevention and the ability to cope with the danger (Johnston and Warkentin 2010; Mwagwabi et al. 2018b).

The coping appraisal Process contains the factors response efficacy, self-efficacy as well as the response costs. Self-efficacy can be defined to as the individuals perception of their own ability to perform the necessary behavior in order to stop the threatening habits. An important role in the center of attention is the individuals' willpower. Self-efficacy is known to have a positive correlation with the intention to adopt protective behavior. It also has a positive affinity with executives' desire to implement anti-malware software (Crossler et al. 2014). PMT means that the probability of activation increases as soon as an end user perceives the recommended response to be valid. There are several studies in the field of ISec researches supporting this. For example, Marett et al. investigated the behavior of social media users. If the latter believe that the deletion of confidential data would contribute to prevent them from being endangered by online threats, they are more willing to not disclose sensitive information. It is likely that users considering suggested security policies may prevent password-based threats are more inclined to obey the recommended policies (Mwagwabi et al. 2018a).

Response efficacy can be defined as the individual's perceived effectiveness of the recommended risk prevention behavior. As with self-efficacy, it has a positive correlation with protection intentions well as with managers' intentions to deploy anti-malware software. A number of related studies (Siponen et al. 2010; Workman et al. 2008) demonstrate the key function of self-efficacy in achieving a substantial reduction in the probability of violations, for example in connection with protection against personal spyware (Johnston and Warkentin 2010), the utilization of social media (Marett et al. 2011) and the securing of personal data (Boss et al., 2015). Users will be more comfortable following the password security recommendations if they are sure they can create a secure password (Mwagwabi et al. 2018a).

Response costs are the expenses which could be referred to as the costs of implementing recommended preventive behavior. This factor decreases the coping appraisal and therefore the protection motivation. As a consequence, high perceived costs could prevent people from participating in recommended behaviors. IS research confirms this by stating that managers' intention to use anti-malware software is reduced when response costs are high (Crossler et al. 2014). Another study by Woon et al (2005) discovered that people who finding wireless security measures at home to be cumbersome are less probable to implement (Woon et al. 2015).

In summary, if the two efficacies explained above are high, the coping appraisal is high as well. If the response costs are high, the coping appraisal is declining. Thus, coping appraisal is the product of self-efficacy and response efficacy minus the response costs. Concluding, the threat appraisal and the coping appraisal lead together to the protection motivation.

2.8.4 Coping Modes

The final element of the PMT approach deals with the question whether a person decides on one or more protective measures and which kind of action is taken. One may distinguish between the adaptive and maladaptive coping modes. The first, adaptive coping mode, is the performance of users to avoid the manifestation of the threat. It is however the choice of the person to not implement the necessary precautionary safety techniques protecting him from the threat. This can be defined as maladaptive coping (Gochman 1997; Lee and Larsen 2009). An example for maladaptive coping strategy would be wishful thinking.

In summary, a person only intends to perform preventive behavior if the individual perceives the severity of a threat, feels vulnerable to that threat, is sufficiently convinced that a particular action will reduce the threat, or feels competent to perform that adequate behavior. If these conditions are complied, a positive purpose is formed. The transformation of an intention into behavior also depends on whether no external barriers or the attitude of caregivers prevent the action. Communication about protection motivation must therefore successfully influence several cognitions, so that a certain endangering behavior changes. Recipients must understand that both the severity of the threat and the likelihood of the danger in question is higher than they previously thought, and that the recommendation contained in the communication is an effective remedy for these serious consequences. Table 1 provides a detailed overview over the cognitive mediating process of the PMT, including all important variables having an effect on protection motivation and the actual change of behavior. Examples on each dimension mentioned above are integrated for a better outlining.

Dimensions	Overview	Examples I´Sec research
Perceived threat severity	Evaluation of seriousness of threat; degree of harm from the behavior	e.g.: people taking password security recommendations when perceiving serious consequences
Perceived threat vulnerability	Assessment of own vulnerability; probability that one will experience harm	e.g.: Probability of a hacker gaining access to personal account
Maladaptive rewards	Positive aspects of starting/continuing behavior	e.g.: restrained continuation for simplicity's sake
Response efficacy	Effectiveness of the recommended behavior in removing/preventing possible harm.	e.g. Effectiveness of anti-malware application
Self-efficacy	Belief that one can successfully execute recommended behavior.	e.g.: Deletion of confidential social media data contributes to preventing online threats
Response costs	Costs associated with the recommended behavior	e.g.: Lower implementation rate of wireless security measures if perceived cumbersome

Table 1: Overview over Variables of Cognitive Mediating Process

2.9   Research done so far

In the past, ISec research concentrated mostly on technical solutions or organizations. However, when researchers began to consider the end user as the weakest link, a shift towards social behavior research ensued (Adams and Sasse 1999).

A number of remarkable studies have therefore included the deduction of the protection motivation theory for this context. The PMT model was primarily used to represent and examine health-related safety habits. Since parallels to preventive behavior in the context of security threats are discernible, researchers from the field of ISec research have applied the protection motivation theory to their research and examined a multitude of security attitudes among individuals or in the context of organizations (Crossler et al. 2014; Vance et al. 2013). The PMT model has most of the time been used to establish a basis for a better understanding of the peoples motivation which has to do with security policy and people managing it. The assumptions and fundamentals of the protection motivation theory are therefore of significant interest for ISec's behavioral science and practice (Chen 2017). There are different approaches to convince people to accept particular actions or ambitions. These motivations involve fear appeals (Boss et al. 2015).

For this reason, contemporary explorations have concentrated on the possible value of fear appeals, based on the PMT, when it comes to enhancing security practices (Mwagwabi et al. 2018a). The question on how to use fear appeals correctly in order to initiate behavioral changes in people while arousing protection motivation among them has occupied researchers for some time now. Scientists have investigated why people react or do not react to a content of a fear appeal in comparison to individuals who are not addressed specifically in the field of ISec and the behavioral security context (Boss et al. 2015; Menard et al. 2017). The PMT model makes use of the fundamentals of fear appeal research by taking dimensions from previous models. These include the two theories described above, in particular the PPM theory. In contrast to the latter theory, which assumes that individuals with maladaptive responses to fear appeals react with ignorance or inactivity, the protection motivation theory includes both reactions, the adaptive and the maladaptive. However, the focus is on adaptive reactions such as protective motivation and the resulting behaviors (Leventhal 1970). The protection mo-tivation theory model states that maladaptive coping behavior has to do with feelings caused by the threat. Therefore, the PMT focuses on adaptive reactions by aiming to motivate people to perform adaptive responses. As a result, the threat can actually be mitigated or even overcome (Chen 2017; Rogers 1975). In summary, PMT has been utilized to describe individuals' tendency to engage in voluntary, safe behavior. Various behavior patterns have been examined at the cause of a better understanding why peo-ple are protecting their assets. Further, it can help to explain why end users who adapt protective behavior are unsuccessful in doing so (Menard et al. 2017).

In order to give a better overview of the adoption of the PMT in the research field of InfoSec, several papers have been reviewed that used studies with derivations and di-mensions of the PMT model. The best results and most valuable articles on information systems can be found in the leading journals (Webster and Watson 2002). The most respected, scientifically proven journals were selected for the literature analysis and formed the basis for a complete coverage of the subject area. In addition to the journals mentioned above, the ECIS and ICIS conferences were researched and reviewed for relevant contributions. For several decades, both of these conferences have been es-tablished gatherings of renowned scientists in the field of information systems ("Confer-ences - Association for Information Systems (AIS)" 2018). The papers were based on various other articles dealing with previous research on this topic and have been ac-cessed through google Scholar, Ebsco Host or Aisel. net. in the time frame from March to June 2018.

30 articles, including their conducted studies, turned out to be appropriate for the current question. The table in the appendix B summarizes the studies found using the dimen-sions of the PMT. This chart contains information on the journals and threat targets within the behavioral context. Furthermore, the table indicates whether only the PMT model was integrated into the study or other models were adopted. If the former was the case, it shows which variables are contained in the construct of the PMT (core and full) and which ones are missing. It is also shown whether fear appeals have been in-cluded. Ultimately, the chart offers a brief overview of the most important results. The overview of the various ISec studies delivers striking insights: The literature and the study results are diverse, contradictory and inconsistent. In the following, outcomings

will be displayed and various reasons where the results may originate from will be presented. Only findings with relevance to the research of this thesis will be named and presented.

First of all most studies have failed to ensure manipulation with fear incentives. Out of 30 papers reviewed, only seven used fear appeal manipulations. One of the few exceptions is the paper by Boss et al. which incorporated fear appeals in form of notifications about the necessity of backups and the use of anti-malware software (Boss et al. 2015). Johnston and Warketing used an appeal of fear to convey the threats of malicious spyware and the impact of user-friendly anti-spyware software to users (Johnston and Warkentin 2010). Another paper, published this year, is the one from Menard et al which addresses fear appeals in the context of password management software (Menard et al. 2017). Therefore, if fear appeals are not applied, one of the core elements of the PMT is missing.

Secondly, most of the studies do not show the correlation between the other dimensions and the behavioral intention as well. Although it´s importance and impact on results is an often held viewpoint, this component is treated differently in various studies (Johnston et al. 2015; Mwagwabi et al. 2018b). Some research studies consider threat as being an autonomous variable (Siponen et al. 2010), while others suggest that fear is a feature of perceived severity and vulnerability (Posey et al. 2015). Some researchers even assume that the three variables are independent and have a direct influence on intentions (Zhang et al. 2009). Comparing results is therefore remains complicated.

Third, the exact role of fear remains unclear in the reviewed studies. The results were found to be very inconsistent. For example, earlier works by Rogers suggest that the fear and the subsequent behavior are directly related. However, it can be seen that different results are also obtained in two different situations. According to the study of Boss et al (data loss on the PC) Boss et al. 2015) or Zhang & McDowell from 2009, the fear of hacking directly influences behavior and plays a significant role in motivating users to take preventive measures. In the organizational environment, however, it appears that fear of protecting the motivation on the company's data assets does not matter. This is shown, for example, by Posey's study in 2015 (Posey et al. 2015) where intentions and actual protection of organization's information assets were measured (Mwagwabi et al. 2018b). This study aims to explore in the personal area, which most of the studies and papers looked at were researching in the personal level as well. Only 12 looked at only the organizational level.

Another conspicuous and fourth point is that for many studies, the core or complete PMT nomology has not been tested and it is not proven that their changes improve the explanatory value of PMT or that the variant model developed or used by the researchers has a more exact match than PMT. Basic variables, contexts and fear appeals are deleted without explanation. Constructs are renamed and measured or even simply omitted. In addition, many of the studies add new constructs that lie outside the nomology of PMT (Boss et al. 2015). The table in the appendix B shows that 18 out of 30 papers looked through added other models or variables besides PMT to test the study. This makes it difficult to measure the results.

Fifth, no study has measured actual fear. Such measurements would help to create an appropriate level of anxiety about the severity of the threat and vulnerability. Therefore, the efficacy cannot be tested exactly. This is because each individual perceives fear at a different level and perceives a threat at different speeds. If fear was measured accurate, this could represent a significant step towards improved research (Boss et al. 2015).

The sixth point is that most studies made very great achievements to behavioral intentions, but dealt very few with the actual behavior of end users. After conducting their study, Boss et al. found that the actual protective behaviors were also carried out at a high fear appeal (Boss et al. 2015). However, in most studies it remains unclear how these so-called appeals for fear may eventually affect the behavior of end consumers (Johnston and Warkentin 2010).

In summary, Boss et al give in their paper four opportunities which could improve the current research. These opportunities are: using the PMT nomology, using fear appeals, measuring fear and measuring actual behavioral changes (Boss et al. 2015).
Finally, IS research concentrates on the immediate effects of fear but does not focus on long term effects (Jenkins et al. 2014; Johnston and Warkentin 2010; Posey et al. 2015; Vance et al. 2013) Mwagwabi et al address this problem, which deals with improving compliance by password guidelines. However, this is also a limitation of this study, since it was prepared within 4 months, making it impossible to measure the long term effects (Mwagwabi et al. 2018b).

3.   Research Model

The primary purpose of this study is to find out whether the induction of fear appeals has an impact on protection motivation relating to protective measures in information sharing and handling own data online. The core question is, if people reconsider their behavior, when they are informed that their personal data is accessible on the internet. This study aims to fill gaps in the literature regarding the impact of fear appeals on the protection motivation from an individual's point of view. Based on indicators of exploratory research, some hypotheses must be formulated a priori. These are evaluated using the construct of an online questionnaire in the following survey and serve to improve the verification and evaluation of the data received from the survey. The protection motivation theory proposes, that the higher the threat, the higher is an individual's behavior to change and adapt its behavior in favor of personal safety activities. Although the literature states that fear appeals should be included in PMT research and ought to be applied within the model, little research conducting fear arousing communications has been applied to date (Boss et al. 2015; Menard et al. 2017). Therefore, in this study, fear appeals are incorporated, in form of potential data leaks. In order to achieve a more expressive and informative result, the survey was divided into two groups. The first group exposed to fear appeals in form of a data leaks in one of their online user accounts based on checking their e-mail address and the second group which did not detect a data leak in one of their user accounts. More information on the fear arousing communication used will be provided in a subchapter in Chapter 4. The hypotheses were formulated in each case for both groups. All relationships between the different variables in the PMT model can be accessed in Figure 3.

As shown in Figure 2, dimensions adding up to the threat appraisal are perceived threat severity and the perceived threat vulnerability. Perceived threat severity can be related to one´s personal concern about the seriousness of the threat (Boss et al. 2015;

Gochman 1997). In this case, perceived severity can be considered as the extent to which a person believes that the consequences of data leaks threats would be harmful. Therefore, the first two hypotheses can be formulated as follows:

H1a: Perceived threat severity in the group exposed to fear appeals in form of potential data leaks will positively influence the factor protection motivation.

H1b: Perceived threat severity in the group not exposed to fear appeals in form of potential data leaks will positively influence the factor protection motivation.

Perceived vulnerability is the personal estimation of the probability of being faced with a specific threat, also standing in positive correlation with the protection intention of an individual (Gochman 1997; Menard et al. 2017). In this thesis, this dimension can be summarized as the extent to which the person exposed believes they are likely to experience threats in regard to data leaks. Therefore, the following hypothesis were proposed:

H2a: Perceived vulnerability to threats in the group exposed to fear appeals in form of potential data leaks will positively influence the factor protection motivation.

H2b: Perceived vulnerability to threats in the group not exposed to fear appeals in form of potential data leaks will positively influence the factor protection motivation.

As mentioned in the section above, fear plays an important role in the protection motivation theory. The term can be defined as the consequence of a threat, in which the affected person is called to negative emotions such as worry or concern. In this case, the individual associates unfavorable feelings with a data leak. Fear can play a mediating function between the threat and the security mechanisms. To trigger fear, people must assume that they are vulnerable to threats (Wall and Buche 2017). In this case, an individual must believe that it would be possible to be personally affected by a data leak in one of the personal user accounts. Another factor to increase fear arises when the individual believes that the consequences of a threat, in this case a data leak, would have serious personal consequences. As a consequence, the following four hypotheses have been presented:

H3a: Perceived vulnerability in the group exposed to fear appeals in the form of potential data leaks is positively related to fear of threat.

H3b: Perceived vulnerability in the group not exposed to fear appeals in the form of potential data leaks is positively related to fear of threat.

H3c: Perceived severity in the group exposed to fear appeals in the form of potential data leaks is positively related to fear of threat.

H3d: Perceived severity in the group not exposed to fear appeals in the form of potential data leaks is positively related to fear of threat.

The factor fear can lead to a user considering protection instructions more severely and as stated above, plays a mediating function between the threat and the intention to engage in more secure behavior (Mwagwabi et al. 2018a). In this case, fear is described as the threat of possible data leaks. Therefore, the following two hypothesis were set:

H4a: An increase of fear in the group exposed to fear appeals in the form of potential data leaks induces an increased motivation for protection.

H4b: An increase of fear in the group not exposed to fear appeals in the form of potential data leaks induces an increased motivation for protection.

Besides the two factors mentioned above, there is a third dimension that directly influences the protection motivation: maladaptive rewards. The latter can be defined as positive aspects of starting or continuing unhealthy behavior (Menard et al. 2017). In this survey, maladaptive rewards are reasons for individuals to continue using weak passwords, for example for reasons of simplicity. For this matter, it is negatively correlated with the protection motivation, and therefore the following hypothesis have been made:

H5a: Increase of maladaptive rewards in the group exposed to fear appeals in the form of potential data leaks are negatively correlated with protection motivation.

H5b: Increase of maladaptive rewards in the group not exposed to fear appeals in the form of potential data leaks are negatively correlated with protection motivation.

According to the protection motivation theory, response efficacy, self-efficacy, and the response costs all together result in the coping appraisal. Response efficacy can be described as an individual's conviction that a proposed reaction will effectively prevent a threat. In this context, if users believe that recommended password policies are able to prevent password-based threats, they are more likely to comply with the recommended policies. Furthermore the PMT model emphasizes, that the increase of response efficacy indicates an advanced likelihood to select the appropriate adaptive response (Boss et al. 2015; Gochman 1997). Therefore, the following hypotheses have been put forward:

H6a: Response efficiency in the group exposed to fear appeals in the form of potential data leaks will positively influence the protection motivation.

H6b: Response efficiency in the group not exposed to fear appeals in the form of potential data leaks will positively influence the protection motivation.

Self-efficacy is the anticipation of an individual's potential to conduct a suggested action (Gochman 1997; Lai et al. 2012). In this case, self-efficacy is described as the degree to which a user has confidence in his personal capacity to generate strong passwords and thus prevent data leaks. As well as response efficacy, self-efficacy is also positively related to the outcome and the adaption of individuals appropriate coping behavior (Gochman 1997). The following hypotheses have been formulated:

H7a: Self-efficacy in the group exposed to fear appeals in the form of potential data leaks will positively influence the protection motivation.

H7b: Self-efficacy in the group not exposed to fear appeals in the form of potential data leaks will positively influence the protection motivation.

Response costs are the perceived expenses of a person in conducting suggested coping actions. In this case, these costs can be defined as the level to which an individual considers it being challenging for him to remember more powerful passwords. Unlike response efficacy and self-efficacy, the response costs have a negative relationship with the likelihood of an individual choosing the appropriate adaptive response (Mwagwabi et al. 2018a). Therefore, this paper hypothesizes:

H8a: Increase of response costs in the group exposed to fear appeals in the form of potential data leaks are negatively correlated with protection motivation.

H8b: Increase of response costs in the group not exposed to fear appeals in the form of potential data leaks are negatively correlated with protection motivation.

When contemplating all these factors, connections and relationships between the variables of the PMT model, it could be suggested, that the greater the strength of a fear appeal manipulation, the stronger the protection motivation and resulting the change of behavior with security related threats. However, in the extent this survey was conducted, it was not possible to create an environment where the actual behavior of end users could be tested in comparison to the protection motivation. This will be explained in more detail later on.

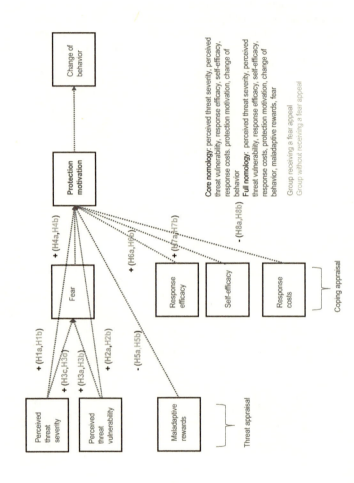

Figure 2: Overview over Hypotheses

4.   Research Method

This chapter outlines the methodological approach of this thesis. Since the aim of this research is to explore and investigate how fear appeals affect the motivating construct and lead to safe behavior on personal information assets, the application of a primarily deductive approach is to be considered in formulating an appropriate and coherent research design as follows. The study design is based on the objectives of the work, which were translated into a guiding question in Chapter 1. The research question, if people reconsider their behavior when they are informed that their data, such as passwords or e-mail addresses, are accessible on the internet is tried to be answered with the conduction of this study. The following study tries to fill gaps existing in literature and research regarding the protection motivation by gaining a more detailed insight concerning fear appeals. Moreover detailed consequences the latter may have on the motivation of individuals with respect to the protection of personal assets were examined.

The following subchapters outline the research design, the developmental characteristics as well as the research design. Furthermore, the website used to arouse fear appeals is presented, followed by detailed information on the fear arousing communication used. Afterwards, the process of collecting data for the core research part of this study is presented, followed by a brief overview over demographic data of the participants.

4.1   Research Design

To ensure that the research design produces results that provide answers to the key question, a quantitative research method was conducted. An online survey questionnaire ("survey data leaks and password security") of quantitative nature served as a central instrument to receive the necessary raw data needed to answer the research question. This method can add breadth to the study enabling to compile data on various aspects from multiple participants. In view of the fact that data protection behavior of private end users on the Internet appeals to a very extensive range of people and thus does not exclude any target group, a quantitative research study was considered to be reasonable.

All participants were informed that their data would be treated anonymously and that neither their names nor other personal information will be published in this thesis. The advantage of this approach is that anonymous questionnaires foster more honest answers than interviews. This represents a suitable technique approaching sensible subjects which could otherwise be considered inappropriate by the respondents during interviews. The emotions and attitudes of the investigated person can be explored in a more detailed and realistic way in a quantitative approach. Furthermore, this type of research provides a logical explanation for observations in a form that could be communicated effectively to others. In addition, quantitative data can easily be plotted on a graph (Burzan 2015).

Also, the questions in the survey conducted were not mandatory, so the respondents decide for themselves which questions they want to answer and for which questions they would rather not give any statement to. This serves to ensure that respondents are more likely to complete the survey. When questions are mandatory, a higher dropout rate can more frequently be observed (Schwartz 2016).

4.2   Development of a Measurement Scale

In order to be able to directly evaluate the protection motivation on privacy, the development of an adequate measurement scale was performed in a multistep process. Concepts and approaches presented within the literature review in combination with the hypothesis formulated in Chapter 3, were taken into account to create questions for the survey.

The questions were formulated on the basis of the PMT model with seven variables. For each subgroup of one dimension there were at least three questions. These can be seen in table 2. In addition, questions from existing research articles were used. An overview of the questions is given in table 3.

	Perceived threat severity
1	A potential data leak could occur with one of my online user accounts.
2	With one of my online user accounts a potential data leak would be serious.
3	With one of my online user accounts, a potential data leak would have significant consequences.
	Perceived threat vulnerability
4	There is a possibility that personal information may be disclosed through a data leak in one of my online user accounts.
5	There is a possibility that personal information may be affected in the future by disclosure due to a data leak.
6	It is unlikely that I will lose data in the future due to a data leak in one of my online user accounts.
	Maladaptive rewards
7	It is more time-saving not to change the passwords of my online user accounts.
8	It is more money-saving not to change the passwords of my online user accounts.
9	The constant change of passwords in my online user accounts confuses me.
10	Due to the constant change of passwords, there is a risk of forgetting the current password.
	Response efficacy
11	Permanent password changes are an effective protection against data theft on one of my online user accounts.
12	Permanent password changes are a good way to protect my data from data theft on one of my online user accounts.
13	By permanently changing passwords I would reduce the possibility of data theft on one of my online user accounts.
	Self-efficacy
14	I am able to protect my personal user accounts from data theft.
15	Protecting my personal user accounts from data theft is a big effort for me.
16	I feel comfortable taking measures to increase the security of my online user accounts.
	Response costs
17	Changing passwords regularly would require too much time.
18	The cost of regularly changing the password reduces the convenience of the application.
19	I do not attach great importance to the regular change of my passwords.

Fear	
20	Potential data leaks are alarming.
21	Data theft could render my online user accounts unusable.
22	I am afraid that one of my online user accounts is affected by data theft.
Protection motivation	
23	I will take precautions in the future to protect my online user accounts from data theft.
24	I intend to change my passwords regularly over the next three months.
25	I predict changing my passwords regularly for the next three months.

Table 2: Overview over Questions asked in Survey in relation to Variables of the PMT

Reference	Question Nr.
What Do Systems Users Have to fear? Using fear appeals to Engender Threats and fear that Motivate Protective Security Behaviors (Boss et al. 2015)	4,5,6,7,8,9,10,12,13,20,21,22
Exploring Factors That Influence Students' Behaviors in Information Security (Yoon et al. 2012)	1,2,3, 11,17,18, 19
Practicing Safe Computing: Message Framing, Self-View, and Home Computer User Security Behavior Intentions (Harrington et al. 2006)	14,16
Fear appeals and Information Security Behaviors: An Empirical Study (Johnston and Warkentin 2010)	15,23,24,25

Table 3: Overview over Literature Review on Questions asked in Survey

4.3   Questionnaire Design

A standardized self-completion online questionnaire was created using the survey tool "Lime Survey" which was modified from the chair of Business Informatics, in particular information systems. The survey contained a total of 32 questions, ensuring an adequate number of questions in regard to the type of survey. The survey was provided in English as well as in German to increase the range of participating persons. The survey could be accessed with a link created specifically for it. The questionnaire allowed a mobile-friendly view as well as a desktop view and could be completed within approximately seven minutes. Responses were accepted from May 19th to July 16th, 2018.

On the first page of the questionnaire, the research topic as well as the goal of the study were introduced. Afterwards, the respondents were asked five brief, demographic questions. The participants introduced themselves by stating their gender, age, nationality, highest level of education as well as their current professional status. Due to the focus laying on a security threat affecting users on a personal level, participants were asked to visit the website *"Have I Been Pwned"* and to enter their e-mail address, which they used most commonly for their personal online user accounts. By pressing "pwned?", the participants were able to check whether a data leak is present in one of their online user accounts. If at least one data leak was indicated, the participant were able to determine on which website their online account was affected by simply scrolling down. After completing the test, the respondent were asked to return to the survey and answer the remaining questions. The first question to be answered was, according to the website, if there is or has been a data leak in one of the personal online user accounts. Another question was if the verified e-mail address is the main e-mail address of the respondent.

The last question, whether the e-mail address tested was the main address of the respondent, due to the researcher having the following concerns:

Most user accounts have only had one e-mail address since a long time. With this specific e-mail address they have signed up for various websites, especially when they were younger, they signed up for questionable sites without second thoughts. When they grew older, they often have acquired a new, more serious e-mail address, with which they do not sign up for as many websites anymore, only for some selected ones. The researcher now had concerns that the evaluation could get falsified due to most user accounts with the "new" e-mail address not showing any data leakage. This is because the new e-mail address was often not used for the registration of various new pages. In addition, a person does not register to new social media sites on a frequent basis, because most registrations were already fulfilled with the old e-mail address.

The researcher had this doubt arising from own experience, as well as from experience of various acquaintances. For this reason, the question of the e-mail address entered was the main e-mail address was inquired. After completion of the survey, however, this could not be confirmed, since 165 of the participants confirmed that the e-mail address was checked, was their main e-mail address.

The last section of the survey consisted of 25 questions exclusively including qualitative items. The questions were divided into three sub-groups which were each displayed on a single page. Sectioning the items was predominantly done for reasons of clarity. The questions can be reviewed in Table 2. Each page showed the percentage of progress in completing the survey. The questions on the last three pages (Q. 8-32) requested the respondent to evaluate using a 7-point Likert scale with 1= Strongly disagree, 2= Disagree, 3= Somewhat disagree, 4= Neither agree nor disagree, 5= Somewhat agree, 6= Agree and 7= Strongly agree. See appendix A for a more detailed description of the questionnaire's design and different sections. A pilot study was performed in advance with a few single individuals acting as potential respondents trying to figure out which parts of the survey still needed to be assimilated. After verification by some people some small functional adjustments were made. Among other things the setting was changed with a separate window opening when the homepage was accessed, due to some participants stating that they could not return to the original questionnaire.

The self-completion questionnaires allowed respondents to revisit questions by going back as long as they did not finally terminate the survey. The tool "Lime Survey" allowed the conductor of the survey to view the number of responses and the submitted answers after completion. The tool did as well record the number of questionnaires that were started but canceled before completion as well as the ones which were filled out incompletely.

4.4   Website "Have I been Pwned"

Hackers break into the servers of large and small online services, stealing usernames, passwords and other details. Many well-known companies and their customers have already been affected. If an individual is a customer of one of these companies, the person wants to know whether his user account belongs to the stolen data as well. It was precisely for these reasons that Troy Hunt launched this site in late 2013 A blog post which was published on its website at the beginning of March 2018 this year is as follows: "*The UK and Australian Governments Are Now Monitoring Their Gov Domains on Have I Been Pwned*" (Hunt 2018).

Troy Hunt is known as Microsoft Regional Director and Most Valuable Professional awardee for Developer Security, international speaker on web security and the author of many top-rating security courses. He created the Website to provide a free tool for anyone to check if the personal online user accounts are affected by possible data leaks. Hunt created this website after the large violation of customer accounts in the case of Adobe in 2013. He states that he designed this site to provide a free service to the public, but also to put a number of technologies to the acid test and to keep his practical skills up to date ("Have I Been Pwned?" n.d.).

The website can be accessed under the following link: https://haveibeenpwned.com/. The name of the side originates from the IT world, and is slang for winning or dominat-ing. It was formed by the misspelling of the word "own" ("Pwned | Define Pwned at Dictionary.Com" 2018). The procedure on the website functions as follows: People can enter their e-mail address or user name, the online service will then tell the individual whether account information has been stolen due to data leaks happened in the past from one of the pages affected. The website obtains this information from the data pro-vided by the hackers after conducting assaults. Boasting about data theft and publishing stolen user names is not uncommon in the scene. In this case, the website can check whether the person is a victim itself. In addition to the direct search on the website, an e-mail service is offered as well: If an individual registers, he will immediately receive a warning by e-mail if the possibility exists to be affected by future incidents. Furthermore, there is a domain search available that allows a person to locate all e-mail accounts on a specific domain that have been caught in any of the currently existing privacy viola-tions. Also, passwords can be entered and checked if they were also affected by data breaches ("Have I Been Pwned?" n.d.).

The website gives an overview about the most important data on data breaches availa-ble on the website. It must be noted, that the numbers have constantly risen since the page was first visited. The last access to the site was on August 10th 2018.

- *300 pwned websites*
- *5,371,008,023 pwned accounts*
- *75,152 pastes*
- *83,039,030 paste accounts*

The top 10 breaches made public on this website are:

- *711,477,622   Onliner Spambot accounts*
- *593,427,119   Exploit.In accounts*
- *457,962,538   Anti Public Combo List accounts*

- *393,430,309   River City Media Spam List accounts*
- *359,420,698   MySpace accounts*
- *234,842,089   NetEase accounts*
- *164,611,595   LinkedIn accounts*
- *152,445,165   Adobe accounts*
- *131,577,763   Exactis accounts*
- *112,005,531   Badoo accounts*

This website groups the data breaches into three groups and assigns them to the individual breaches. The three different dimensions are:

- Sensitive breach, not publicly searchable
- Unverified breach, may be sourced from elsewhere
- Spam List, used for spam marketing

4.5   Survey: Fear-Appeal Manipulation

In order to verify the hypotheses fairly, the presence of fear appeals was necessary. Two groups were formed due to better measuring of the effects: one group that did not experience fear appeals and one group being exposed to fear appeals. The study did not, as in most other studies conducted so far, assign the groups beforehand. The participants of the groups were assigned as follows. After answering the demographic questions, it was obligatory for all participants to visit the above-mentioned website and find out whether a data leak occurred in one of the personal user accounts to date. Depending on the answer, the groups were then assigned to the two groups. Attendants who noticed a data leak up to date belonged to the group with the fear appeals. The remaining participants, the group of people who did not have to deal with a data leak of their personal user accounts, consequently belonged to the group without receiving fear appeals. Both groups had to answer the same questions in the course of the further survey. The researcher divided the two groups when accessing the raw data in SPSS and carried out the analyses twice: once for the group with fear appeals and the same evaluation for the group without fear appeals. In the following, the evaluations for the two groups were considered separately. Furthermore, it is important to note that it cannot be hypothesized automatically no fear appeal condition being assumed for the group not suffering from data leaks. Boss et al. state, that fear appeals may not only be caused by data leaks from e-mail addresses, as tested on the special homepage, but can also be triggered by different scenarios. However, this is an unusual occasion and was therefore neglected for the study carried out (Boss et al. 2015). It can be assumed that fear appeals have a significant influence on the perceived fear of using stronger passwords in the future or of changing them more frequently. Therefore, it was important to form to groups in order to have a better comparison of the influence of fear appeals on the variables in the PMT. This results in simplifications in the analysis followed in the next chapter. Actual occupations will be explained in more detail later on.

4.6   Data Collection

This study was carried out with an online link which the participants could open on any device. For reaching potential attendees, personal networking with friends, fellow students from the university, colleagues from work and other acquaintances was practiced. The aim was to predominantly contact potential respondents directly, in order to create a higher rate of response.

As mentioned above, an English alternative of the questionnaire was created as well, in order to extend the range of participants and contact acquaintances from oversee and other non-German-speaking countries. Additional public requests in Facebook groups supported the reach of potential candidates. Furthermore, the researcher has joined several other groups which are concerned with the mutual exchange of participations in surveys.

4.7   Participants

The majority of people are actively on the Internet and social media every day either on their computer, mobile phone, tablet or any other device. Therefore a large mass of people is constantly exposed to the danger of violating privacy and loss of data. Since the topic can affect anyone, the candidates where chosen without fulfilling any specific required criteria. The study was not assigned to a specific target group.

Out of the 284 who participated in the survey, 265 people stated their age. The sample consisted of respondents ranging from 15 to 58 years and the average age of those questioned was 25,83. and had at least a High School Diploma. Their current professional status ranged from being pupils, students or employees, with most of the participants being be enrolled at a university (69,4%). Out of the participants 169 were female (59,5%) and 96 were male (33,8%). 19 participants did not state their gender (6,7%). The sample consisted of 33 different nationalities which German the most widely represented nationality with 194 of all respondents (68,3%). On the demographic questions, only gender and age were the only questions not fully answered. Nationality, highest level of education and current professional statues were fully answered. The language the survey was filled out was German for 217 people (76,4 %) and 67 respondents answered the questionnaire in English (23,6%). Out of the respondents, 100 people, which adds up to 35,2%, stated that there is a data leak on one of their online user accounts according to the website. 125 (44 %) stated, there was no data leak in their online user accounts. 59 respondents (20,8%) did not give a response. Furthermore, 184 (64%) stated that the e-mail address they checked was their main e-mail address. 41 participants (14,4%) only stated, that the e-mail address they checked was not their main e-mail address.

5.   Results

This chapter reveals valuable results provided through the analysis of the answers made disposable by the questionnaire. First, the measurement validity of the study is pointed out by outlining the examinations done. Afterwards, the procedure for the evaluation is described. In order to appraise the raw data correctly so that the hypotheses can be reliably answered according to the results, a multiple linear regression was considered appropriate. Multiple linear regression is a special case of the general linear model by which influences of predictors (variables used to predict the values of other variables) on a criterion can be studied, in this case the different predictors on protection motivation. This allows to determine whether the correlation of two variables are found statistically significant. Furthermore, future values can be predicted with the help of this regression (Kaul 2014).

The steps after examination lead to the inspection of the verification of the hypotheses by examining the significant effects between the individual variables. Afterwards, a short overview of the evaluations is presented. Recommendations for actions on the basis of the results are presented in the discussion.

5.1   Measurement Validity

A central result of the reliability analysis is Cronbach's Alpha. This coefficient is a measure of the reliability, more precisely the reliability of the overall scale and also often referred to as the measure of internal consistency. Cronbach´s Alpha is not the result of a statistical test but a simple coefficient, in the following also abbreviated with CA. If a scale measures the quantity of interest free of systematic errors, the individual observed values will differ due to two effects. First, the values vary because the measured size has different characteristics for the different objects observed. Second, in addition to the quantity to be considered, random errors are also reflected in the measurement errors. In conclusion, the total variance is composed of the inherent variance and the total one. Therefore, the reliability of a scale is defined as the proportion of inherent variance in the total variance (Brosius 2011; Eckstein 2016). The reliability of a scale is usually not easy to determine. After the measurement of a quantitative study is complete, one usually only has the observed values, but the true values or the size of the errors are unknown. It is therefore considered difficult to determine how the total variance is divided between inherent variance and error variance. In the case of a composite scale, like in this thesis however, trustworthy statements can be made about the reliability. Cronbach's alpha is larger the higher the validity of the whole scale is. If the individual variances have identical variances and error ones, Cronbach's alpha is an accurate estimate of the reliability, otherwise it indicates the lower limit of the reliability of the entire scale (Brosius 2011). The value of this ratio can range between 0 and 1, with a high value indicating high reliability and a lower value indicating a lower one. According to Nunnally (1978), only values exceeding 0.7 can be accepted. Because the amount of the value depends on the number of indicators, different values are assumed for different indices. For a measuring instrument consisting of two indicators a value of 0.5 is accepted, whereas for 3 indicators a value of 0.6 is satisfactory (Herr 2007). Therefore, considering the structure of the conducted study, a value of more than 0.6 was considered reliable for this evaluation.

The measurement of the individual variables yielded to the following results and can be reviewed in the Appendix D in more detail. The CA amount for protection motivation theory is $\alpha=0,67$, for vulnerability $\alpha=0,59$, and for maladaptive rewards, CA amounts to $\alpha=0,71$. Response efficacy subscribes a CA value of $\alpha=0,91$. Self-efficacy, however, has a very low amount of only $\alpha= 0,25$. For the response costs the value was $\alpha=0,66$ and for fear, Cronbach´s alpha is $\alpha=0,63$. For the last variable, protection motivation, the CA value equals $\alpha=0,90$. The CA results for the variables perceived threat severity, maladaptive rewards, response efficacy, response costs, fear and protection motivation were acceptable. However, some of the above measured values were lower than expected, namely vulnerability and self-efficacy. Notwithstanding, there are some approaches to explain the low values: Since Cronbach's Alpha evaluates whether the composition of the individual variables can be considered reasonable or not, after testing the CA values the compilations of the individual questions contained in the survey were examined again in more detail. After assessment of the questions referring to the two variables, one thing has caught the eye: All other questions of the survey were formulated in a positive way, but vulnerability and self-efficacy included two negative formulated questions. Vulnerability first asked participants whether there was a possibility that personal information could be disclosed through a data leak in one of the personal online user accounts, in the present or the future. This was followed by the question of whether it is considered unlikely that a data leak could lead to data loss. This last question was formulated negatively which is an indication of the low CA value. The same applies for the variable self-efficacy: After the question whether the person assesses to be able to protect the personal user accounts against data theft, the statement followed that protecting user accounts against data theft is connected with great effort for the individual. Then followed another positively formulated question that one feels comfortable taking measures to increase the security of personal online user accounts. Since Cronbach's alpha looks how similar the variables are in relation to the answers of the participants, this is an indication for the low CA value of the two variables. In addition, since the probability of misleading wording of the questions it is likely that the questions confused the participants or that they did not read those questions correctly. This can explain that the answers of the participants for these two variables lie very far apart on the Likert-scale. This explains the low CA value. For self-efficacy, this number is probably even lower, since the question was posed between two questions formulated in a positive way.

5.2   Data Analysis

The aim of this study is to gain a comprehensive understanding for the impact of fear appeals on protection motivation of internet users in connection with data leaks on personal user accounts. The methods of analysis presented in this chapter have been considered in terms of their suitability and their importance for the development of a desirable and adequate understanding of the results of this research.
The raw data of the responses of the survey conducted was downloaded in a .csv-file. Another .sps-file was retrieved containing the syntax. The data was then processed and assessed in SPSS 25 and Excel. In addition, some results and statistics could be retrieved from the tool of the university chair itself. An overview for the German as well as the English version over the statistics was downloaded and handed in separately with this thesis. The evaluation procedure was has progressed as follows: First, the two data sets, the German and the English one, were merged into one large common file in SPSS. Missing cases for filter queries after data leakage were then generated. Afterwards, some of the values had to be recoded, resulting in an easier interpretation of the results (Hatzinger and Nagel 2009). After completing these tasks, an entire data set was ultimately generated.
Afterwards, in order to summarize the proceedings done with SPSS, the data of the questionnaire was divided into two different groups: the group with fear appeals and the

groups without fear appeals. The first group assayed, was the one which received the fear appeals, in other words, the groups where there was found at least one data leak in one of the participants e-mail user accounts. Thereafter, the rest of the questionnaire, the group with none of their e-mail address having a data leak was looked at more closely. All executions were carried out with the two factors that have a direct effect on the variable fear, namely perceived threat severity and perceived threat vulnerability. Then, all other variables were associated with protection motivation. At the beginning of the calculations, maladaptive rewards were not executed, which was calculated separately at the end, due to the test of multicollinearity. However, this will be explained in more detail below.

Descriptive statistical analysis indicators, such as mean and standard deviation, served as tools to summarize frequencies and simplify outcomes. This subsequently allows a comparison to other studies that for example surveyed similar or the same motivational items. Those values can be found in Appendix D.

Also the valid and the excluded answers of the questionnaires are listed in the output.

The sample size comprised 284 completed surveys, of which 73 were only partially answered or were canceled during execution. 217 of the respondents completed the survey in German, 67 of them conducted the survey in English. After subtracting the partially answered questionnaires, 162 exploitable data sheets remain for the German version and 49 for the English one. This results in 211 totally completely answered questionnaires. After assessing the data with SPSS and including all the exploitable data sheets, even though they were not completely answered, 225 questionnaires remained for exploration. For some calculations, some further data sheets were dismissed. Therefore, the spreadsheets executed ranged from 207 to 214 in the different scenarios.

In order to avoid a non-distortion in the evaluation, only questionnaires were included in the evaluation which have completely been filled out or where the respondents have at least completed the majority starting from the question whether there was a data leak in the personal user account. In the overview of the participants, such as demographic data, the questionnaires not being filled out completed the entire survey were also included in the overview which can be found in the Appendix C.

Furthermore, the Pearson coefficient can also be considered and looked at in the output. A dimensionless measure of the degree of linear relationship between two at least interval-scaled characteristics. It can have values between −1 and +1. With a value of 1 there is a completely positive linear relationship between the characteristics under consideration. These values can be viewed more detailed in the appendix for the different scenarios (Shevlyakov and Oja 2016).

Before the results of the regression analysis were dissected, the prerequisites should be checked. After testing Cronbach's Alpha, the variables formed were now checked for multicollinearity. This term describes a linear dependence between two or more independent variables which means that two or more explanatory variables have a very strong correlation with each other. This is a central problem in regression-based statistical analyses and could, among other things, have a negative impact on the model's informative value. The reviews show that maladaptive rewards have a high multicollinearity to the variable response costs. In relation to this study, it can be said that the answers in these two dimensions were almost congruent. However, a certain multicollinearity is entirely normal and the model can still be considered valid (Albers 2009).

Since both cases have been under examination, and the results including the maladaptive rewards were observed without major changes on the values, this variable was ultimately kept during the analysis in order to not distort the theoretical results and the verification of the hypotheses.

Next, the model quality was checked. The so-called "R-square" is also referred to as "measure of determination". It shows how well the estimated model fits the data collected and how well it elucidates variance. The coefficient of determination expresses the share of the variance declared by the independent variable in the total variance of the dependent variable square describes what proportion of the scatter in the dependent variable can be explained by the independent variables. It grows with increasing number of explanatory variables r^2 can take values between 0 and 1. 0 means that the model has no explanatory power, 1 states that the model can perfectly predict the observed values. The higher the r^2 value, the better the fit between model and data (Baur and Fromm 2008). Since the normal r^2 overestimates the explanatory power to some extent, another corrected r^2 is output (Jannsen and Laatz 1999). In this case, the adjusted r square for the group with fear appeals looks as follows: 0 ,275 for all variables on protection motivation and 0,302 for the two variables on fear. For the group without fear appeals, the results look as follows: for the groups with a fear appeal, 0,451 for the groups without no fear appeals on all variables and 0,51 as well for the two remaining variables that affect fear. The Adjusted R2 seem legit because one can speak in the interpretation of a medium or medium-strong effect.

Next, the Durbin Watson statistics can be displayed. This coefficient provides information about a possible autocorrelation of the residua, i.e. whether the correlation between two successive residual variables in a regression analysis is not zero. The closer the value of the coefficient is to 2, the lower the degree of autocorrelation. Values well below 2, on the other hand, point to a positive autocorrelation, values well above 2 to a negative autocorrelation (Baur and Fromm 2008). The value amount is 1,575 for the groups with fear appeals and 1,226 for the one without any data leaks. The results therefore state, that for both groups, no autocorrelation is present. Therefore, the two values which are present in this study seem legitimate.

After considering the prerequisites, the significance of the overall regression model was now considered. An analysis of variance, or ANOVA, was performed. The sum of squares are set in relation to the degrees of freedom, the means of the square sums are calculated and checked for significance with an F-test. This examines whether the prediction of the dependent variable is improved by adding the independent variable. This means that the F-Test checks whether the model makes an overall explanation contribution. ANOVA significance was for all four cases 0,000 so the model overall is highly significant. The model is thus validated.

SPSS now checked whether the regression coefficients (β) are also significant. A t test is performed for each of the regression coefficients. The results of the t-test can be viewed in the columns "T" and "Sig.". from table 4 to 7 and in the appendix D.1-D.4 for the different scenarios. The t-test checks whether two of the regression coefficients are significantly different from zero in the population (Brosius 2013).

In order to verify the validity of the individual hypotheses, the β need to be consulted. Betas are the standardization of coefficients, i.e. they are scale invariant. This means that they no longer depend on the original predictor scales. Only betas for which a significance has been determined are considered for evaluation. If the value of a variable would change one standard deviation up or down, then the dependent variable, i.e. protection motivation, would change by exactly this beta value (Kaul 2014).

In summary, all the processes described above can be viewed in more detail in Appendix a to c. Among other things, histograms, normal p-p plot of standardized residual and the partial regression plot are displayed. The first two give a useful impression of whether the data we analyze is largely normally distributed. The histogram usually allows a very good estimation of whether variables are normally dispersed. In the P-P diagram, the observed residuals are plotted against the expected standardized ones. For normal distribution, the values should be on the diagonals shown. The partial regression plot shows a graphical representation of the regression line (Krentz 2009). From the illustrations it can be seen that almost exclusively all histograms represent a normal distribution. Some of them are slightly different, although this is not unusual in terms of the number of participants. Also the partial regression plot does not show any big deviations. For the last one, the P-P diagram, can be seen, that there are also no big discrepancies to see. Therefore, the conditions for a multiple linear regression are fulfilled.

In the In the following section, the hypotheses are tested on the basis of the interpretation of the significance and the standard beta coefficients. Furthermore, all the above statistics and tables can be viewed in detail in the appendix D.1-D.4.

5.3   Group Results

This chapter reveals valuable results provided through the analysis of the evaluated questionnaires.

Tables 4-7 give an overview of the results obtained from group 1 and 2, the group with the persons who did not experience a fear appeal. As can be read from the table, for the group without an experience of a data leak, four relationships, which makes 44,44 %, state significant effects, namely: threat severity on fear, fear on protection motivation, self-efficacy on protection motivation and response costs to protection motivation.

No significance was found for the remaining , namely vulnerability on fear, maladaptive rewards on protection motivation, response efficacy on protection motivation, threat severity on protection motivation as well as vulnerability on protection motivation.

For the group directed a fear appeal to, where an existing data leak in one of the personal e-mail accounts occurred look a little different: significance was found in two cases which makes 22,22 %. The relationships for which was found a significant relationship are threat severity on fear and fear on protection motivation. No significant effects are existing for self-efficacy on protection motivation and response costs to protection motivation vulnerability on fear, maladaptive rewards on protection motivation, response efficacy on protection motivation, threat severity on protection motivation as well as vulnerability on protection motivation. The procedure for reviewing the hypotheses is as follows: First of all, the significance was looked at. In statistics, the following three significance levels or limits are generally used: When $p \leq 0.05$ the correlation is significant, which means that errors are probability less than 5 % and SPSS assigns an asterisk = *. For $p \leq 0.01$ the relationship is very significant, so the errors are probability of error less than 1 % and SPSS assigns 2 stars **. If p ≤ 0.001 very high significant correlations exist, so the errors are probability less also than 1 % SPSS assigns 3 stars *** (Schuchmann 2016). After having a look at the significant relationships among the variables of the PMT, the Standardized Coefficients Beta are looked. The β-coefficients are required for the prediction. However, this factor only has an influence and was only considered if there is a significance present. The higher the value of β, the higher the relationship between the individual variables. A value of 0.1 to 0.2 is considered weak. Up to 0.4 states a medium correlation and afterwards strong to very strong correlations are present. On this foundation, the hypotheses and the strength of the of the individual connections can be tested. The following tables show an overview of the different values needed in order to examine the hypotheses.

Coefficients no Data Leak on Fear					
Model	Unstandardized Coefficients		Standardized Coefficients	t	Sig.
	B	Std. Error	Beta		
1 (Constant)	1,670	,353		4,728	,000
p_threats	,283	,087	,328	3,269	,001
vulnerb	,165	,117	,141	1,404	,163

Table 4: Overview over Coefficients no Data Leak on Fear

Coefficients no Data Leak on Protection Motivation					
Model	Unstandardized Coefficients		Standardized Coefficients	t	Sig.
	B	Std. Error	Beta		
1 (Constant)	3,316	,528		6,284	,000
fear	,512	,108	,394	4,729	,000
res_cost	-,549	,110	-,506	-5,005	,000
self_effi	,268	,125	,166	2,148	,034
res_effi	,122	,094	,106	1,300	,196
mala_rew	-,019	,121	-,017	-,156	,876
p_threats	,063	,098	,056	,638	,525
vulnerb	-,071	,135	-,047	-,524	,601

Table 5: Overview over Coefficients no Data Leak on Protection Motivation

Coefficients Data Leak on Fear					
Model	Unstandardized Coefficients		Standardized Coefficients	t	Sig.
	B	Std. Error	Beta		
1 (Constant)	,814	,411		1,980	,051
p_threats	,496	,097	,491	5,100	,000
vulnerb	,201	,143	,136	1,410	,162

Table 6: Overview over Coefficients Data Leak on Fear

Coefficients Data Leak on Protection Motivation					
Model	Unstandardized Coefficients		Standardized Coefficients	t	Sig.
	B	Std. Error	Beta		
1 (Constant)	1,742	,814		2,141	,035
fear	,698	,183	,472	3,815	,000
res_cost	-,254	,154	-,200	-1,656	,101
self_effi	,015	,204	,008	,075	,940
res_effi	,225	,118	,197	1,903	,060
mala_rew	,018	,177	,013	,104	,917
p_threats	-,036	,172	-,024	-,209	,835
vulnerb	,002	,221	,001	,010	,992

Table 7: Overview over Coefficients Data Leak Data Leak on Protection Motivation

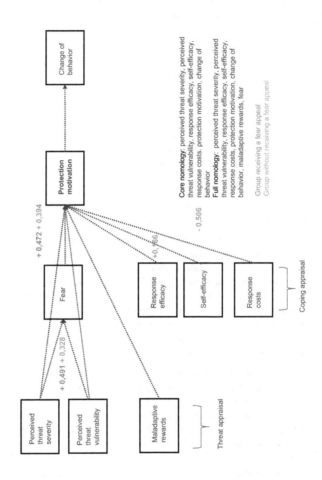

Figure 3: Overall Model Results for Survey

The following results were obtained for the threat perception hypotheses: In order to test hypotheses, a brief review of their statements must be made.

Hypothesis 1a prophesied the positive correlation between the protection motivation theory of the threat in the group exposed to fear appeals and the influence on the factor of protection motivation. Hypothesis 1b predicted the same, but related to the group of people who did not receive a fear appeal. After the regression was made, following results were obtained: the significance for the group with fear appeals was p= 0,835 and without fear appeals p= 0,525. The Standardized Coefficients Beta is β= 0,024 for the group receiving a fear appeal and β= 0,056 for the group without fear appeals. Since for both groups there is no significant effect present, hypothesis H1a and H1b are not substantiated.

Hypothesis 2a and Hypothesis 2b stand for the positive relationship between he perceived vulnerability to threats in the group exposed to fear appeals and in the group not exposed to fear appeals will positively influence the motivation for protection. The results of the investigations were as follows: p= 0,601 for the group without fear appeals and p= 0,992 for the group with fear appeals. The correlation is therefore not significant and no statements can be made for the relationships. The standardized coefficient beta is β= 0,001 for the group receiving four arousing communication and β= -0,047 for the group not being exposed to fear appeals. Due to no significant effects being present, hypotheses H2a and H2b are unfounded.

Furthermore, perceived vulnerability is positively related to fear of a threat. This is stated by the Hypothesis 3a and Hypothesis 3b. This applies to the group exposed to fear appeals as well as to the group not exposed to fear appeals.
The correlation is not significant. This can be read from the following results: the significance for the group with fear appeals was p= 0,162 and without fear appeals p= 0,163. The relationship can therefore be considered not significant. The standardized coefficient beta is β = 0,141 for the group receiving a fear appeal and β= 0,136 for the group without an receiving a fear arousing communication. For this reason the hypotheses H3a and H3b are not valid, due to no testimony can be made.

Hypothesis 3c and Hypothesis 3d stand for the positive relationship between he perceived severity to threats in the group exposed to fear appeals and in the group not exposed to fear appeals will positively influence the fear of the threat. The results of the investigations were as follows: p= 0,000 for the group with fear appeals and p= 0,001 for the group without fear appeals. The standardized coefficient beta is β= 0,491 for the person receiving a fear arousing communication and β= 0,328 for the person without receiving any. For the group with fear appeals, the following scenario applies: At a level of significance of 100 %, there is a strong positive correlation between perceived severity and protection motivation of 0,491. Concluding, if the perceived severity raises by one scale point, motivation intention increases by 0,491, under the condition of all other variables remaining constant. At a significance level of 99%, there is a medium positive correlation between perceived severity and protection motivation of 0,328. This means that if perceived severity increases by one scale point protection motivation raises by 0.328 on the assumption that that all other variables remain constant. For this reason the hypotheses H3c and H3d are justifiable.

In the investigations between the relationship of fear and protection motivation, the following results were obtained: p= 0,000 for the group without fear appeals and p= 0,000 for the group with fear appeals. Hypothesis 4a and 4b forecast a positive correlation between fear and motivation for protection, for the group with fear appeals as well as for the group without fear appeals. According to the results, for both groups, the relationship between the two variables is significant. The standardized coefficient beta is β= 0,472 for the persons receiving a fear appeal and β= 0,394 for the persons without. For this reason the hypotheses H4a and H4b are valid.

For the group receiving fear arousing communication applies the following: At a level of significance of 100% there is a strong positive correlation between fear and protection motivation of 0,472. Under the assumption that that all other variables remain constant, fear increases by one scale point if protection motivation raises by 0,472. For the group without fear appeals, can be stated: at a significance level of 100% there is a medium positive correlation between fear and protection motivation of 0,394. When all other variables remain constant, fear increases by one scale point if protection motivation raises by 0,394.

Therefore it is not surprising that the connection between the factor of maladaptive rewards and the protection motivation looks like this: p= 0,876 for the group without fear appeals and p=0,917 for the group with fear appeals.

Therefore, Hypothesis 5a and b, which stated a negative correlation between maladaptive rewards and protection intention cannot be supported. The standardized coefficient beta is β= -0,013 for the person receiving a fear arousing communication and β= -0, 17 for the group without fear appeals. Due to for both groups, the relationship between maladaptive rewards and protection motivation not being significant, the hypotheses H5a and H5b are unfounded.

Hypothesis 6a and Hypothesis 6b state that perceived response efficacy in the group exposed to fear appeals will positively influence the protection motivation. The same goes for the group which did not get exposed to fear appeals. The results from the study are as follows: p= 0,060 for the groups with data leaks exposed and p= 0,196. No significance is shown which leads to the hypothesis not being supported. The standardized coefficient beta is β= 0,197 for the group receiving a fear appeal and β= 0,106 for the person without having a data leak. Therefore, no significant correlation between the two variables are present. Concluding, the hypotheses H6a and H6b are unfounded.

Next, the relationship between perceived self-efficacy in the group exposed to fear appeals as well as in the group not exposed to fear appeals will positively influence the protection motivation. This states the hypothesis 7a as well as 7b. These Hypothesis were confirmed as the correlation were significant. This observation derived from the following results: p= 0,034 for the group not receiving a fear appeal and p= 0,940. The standardized coefficient beta is β= 0,008 for the person receiving a fear appeal and β= 0,166 for the persons without a data leak. For this reason the hypotheses 7b is justifiable, due to having a significant relationship. But there is no significance found for the group with fear appeals so and H7a stays unfounded.

The last hypotheses, the H8a und H8b state that the increase of response costs in the group exposed to fear appeals are negatively correlated with protection motivation. This takes into account for the groups with fear appeals as well as the groups without fear appeals. P= 0,101 in the group with fear appeals as well as p= 0,000 for the group without fear appeals. The standardized coefficient beta is β= -0,200 for the persons receiving a fear appeal and β= -0,506 for the person without a fear arousing communication. No significant effects were found for the group receiving a fear appeal. Therefore, no statement can made about Hypothesis 8a, H8b however is found valid. At a significance level of 100% there is a strong negative correlation between response costs and the intention to perform protective behavior of -0,506. When all other variables remain constant, response costs decrease by one scale point if protection motivation diminishes by -0,506.

6.   Discussion

Building on the previous chapters, this current section focuses on interpreting and discussing the findings of Chapter 5 by relating to aspects outlined in Chapter 2 and 3. On this basis, and in line with the idea of an deductive research approach, the results of the study will be discussed and the outcome of the hypotheses tested will be examined. The presented findings of the survey conducted in this paper serve as a basis for reflecting upon possible theoretical themes and formulating deriving theories. Relations between aspects surveyed were outlined in the previous chapter. Looking at the relationships between the individual variables of the protection motivation theory, which emerge from the combination of theoretical foundations with the results of systematic literature analysis, it becomes apparent that most of them cannot be confirmed in the context of practical application.

Although, based on strategic literature analysis conducted for the theoretical background and studies evaluated before, a fully supported PMT model would have been expected. However, in the practical study conducted for this thesis, the protection motivation model did not hold. Various variables dropped out, due to no significant effects could get verified. These variables for both groups in relation to protection motivation were: perceived threat severity, perceived threat vulnerability, maladaptive rewards and response efficacy.

For the group receiving a fear arousing communication, response costs and self-efficacy dropped out as well. In regard to the relationships variables, directly influencing fear, the following results can be obtained: for both groups, the vulnerability showed no significance and therefore was dismissed as well. In addition, vulnerability falsely decreased the protection motivation for the group without data leaks and perceived threats also decreased the correlation for the group with data leaks. Also, maladaptive rewards stated a false positive relationship to protection motivation in the group without fear appeals.

Concluding, the sample data deviates strongly from a pre-determined assumption that this presumption get discarded according to a predetermined rule.

Regarding the ANOVA table which showed that the model was being significant overall, most variables not having significant effects needs further enquiry.

Concluding, the following indications were made: the size of the sample collected may have been too small in order to assess all relationships on the variables present. Even though there were 284 respondents to the survey, only 207 to 214 data sheets were considered exploitable. Therefore, more collected data may be necessary.

Furthermore, it can be concluded, that the fear appeal was not strong enough to arouse an appropriate level of fear. This statement can be inferred when the results of this study are compared to the ones from Boss et al.. In their two studies conducted, they made a differentiation between low and strong fear appeals. In the first scenario, the model with lower fear arousing communications did not hold as well and showed almost no significant effects between the individual variables. When the fear appeal was increased however, significant effects were shown for all variables. When regarding the r^2 for the study receiving high fear incentives, r^2 takes a value of 0,881 (Boss et al. 2015). In comparison to the study conducted for this thesis, the r^2 output was approved valid by the researcher before the evaluation because of stating a medium correlation. To review this, the r^2 for this study for the group of fear appeals valued 0,302 for the perceived threat severity and perceived vulnerability on fear. R^2= 0,275 for the correlation of the remaining variables on protection motivation. For the group without fear appeals the r^2 put out the following results: 0,451 for all variables on protection motivation and very low value of 0,161 for the two remaining variables on fear. In relation to the paper from Boss et al., these may be the reason why almost no significant effects were present. In order to confirm this statement made, the highest r^2 in this study can be reviewed: the value of 0,451 for the remaining variables on protection motivation has established the most significant relationships.

Another conclusion can be drawn from the paper published by Boss et al.: The results state, that a higher threat is perceived when fear appeals are posed at individuals more often (Boss et al. 2015). However in the study conducted for this thesis, there was only one single fear appeal directed at the individuals. Results may have differed if fear appeals were received more than once.

If the remaining hypotheses are considered, for the relationships in the group without any fear appeals, four hypotheses were valid due to significant effects being found. The positive relationship between protection motivation theory on the variable fear, the positive relationship between fear as well as self-efficacy an protection motivation, and the negative relationship of response costs to protection motivation. For the group with fear appeals, the positive relationship of threat severity on fear and also the positive relationship of fear on protection motivation showed significant effects. Furthermore, to answer the research question, it is important to consider the effect of fear appeals on each variables. Here it is noticeable, that in the group with data leaks the fear appeals have a strong effect on the protection motivation (β= 0, 472) in comparison to the group without receiving fear appeals which only results in a medium effect on protection motivation (β = 0,394). Also the output for perceived threat severity show the same: Beta was stating a strong effect in the group with a data leak a data leak being present (β = 0,491) whereas for the group without fear appeals the beta showed that a medium effect between perceived threat severity and fear is existing (β= 0,328). The other two hypothesis cannot be considered in this discussion, due to them only being significant for the group without experiencing a data leak.

Concluding, even though the model did not hold, the assumption of fear appeals having an observable effect on different variables of the PMT and therefore on protection motivation can be stated from the two connections shown above.

Those findings will be discussed in more detail in the following sections. They provide implications, not only of theoretical origin but of practical terms as well. The implications aim to underline the statements described in the previous chapter and tries to draw conclusions for giving further implications to the reader. The theoretical implications offer an aggregated outline about the current knowledge in the area of fear appeals on protection motivation. The practical implications are offering a guideline of how to successfully improve the research in the field of privacy in ISec research. The sector of limitations offers restrictions of the described theoretical background and depicts in which way the quantitative study as well as the theoretical background are limited.

6.1   Theoretical Implications

This research examined emerging gaps in the usage of fear appeals. Only very little literature sparse research is existing regarding the application of fear arousing communication while adopting the protection motivation theory. Also it shows a lot of inconsistency of the results. The study of Johnson Warketing conducted in the year 2010 is the first of its kind to investigate this phenomenon and is mentioned in the current literature or the foremost of its nature to be found when looking through the articles (Johnston and Warkentin 2010). The ensuing investigation by Boss et al. initially shaped the fear appeal research by conducting two studies with different levels of fear arousing communication (Boss et al. 2015). Also the relatively new study from Menard et al. did the same, inducting fear appeals within the research (Menard et al. 2017). Fear arousing communications are part of the core functions that lead to a proper PMT application in ISec research. Not using fear appeals leads to potentially false and misleading results (Boss et al. 2015). The present paper aims to close existing gaps within the research of privacy and extend the existing knowledge about fear appeals. The findings within this research study, offer several contributions to already existing examinations on the concept of fear appeals already examined in Chapter 2.9. The results of the study confirm what was predicted earlier in the literature research on PMT:

First, it is important to use fear appeal manipulations in science which was already stated by many researchers (Boss et al. 2015; Mwagwabi et al. 2018b) . The specially for this thesis conducted study confirms that the fear arousing communications which were directed at the participants in the form of potential data leaks have had an observable effect. As stated in the previous chapter, hypothesis 3c and 3d, the positive relationship between perceived severity on fear were justified. The same holds true for H4a and H4b, which predicted positive relationship between fear and protection motivation. Due to both variables having a stronger effect in the group which received a fear appeal, the relevance of fear appeals in research are confirmed. Thus, in the future, the usage fear appeals should be continued in the research to obtain a correct outcome and evaluation of the studies.

Second, another point figured out while evaluating the research done so far is, that the majority of the studies disagree about the relationships between the individual variables (Mwagwabi et al. 2018b; Posey et al. 2015; Siponen et al. 2010; Zhang et al. 2009). In this study, the variables had the following connections: perceived threat severity and vulnerability were both having a relationship with fear and protection motivation. The remaining variables were all stated to have a direct relationship to the intention to conduct preventive behavior. Even though, not all relationships were found significant, it can be assumed that with a higher fear appeal, most connections would have been had significant effects. Concluding, further research should use a unified adaption of relationships between the variables. A standardized model would promote consistent outcomes and provide enormous assistance for further interpretation.

The third implication proposed by this thesis can be related to the amount and measurement of fear. The quantitative nature of the study outlines the importance of using the right amount of fear in future research. According to this questionnaire conducted, which provided a reasonable amount of fear, can be seen that this amount of fear arousing communication was appropriate to trigger the motivation to change the passwords in the future. Notwithstanding, a higher fear appeal would probably have found significant effects among the remaining variables. This can also be deduced by the paper Boss et al.: study results show that manipulations with a high fear incentive generate more fear and supportive threat that stimulates protection motivation than manipulations with a low fear incentives. The paper also proves, that with higher fear communication valid results are achieved than models containing lower fear appeals, especially when it comes to influencing actual behavior (Boss et al. 2015).

The next implication also to depends on the previous one. The studies looked at, hardly any of the researchers ever measured the real amount of fear (Boss et al. 2015). This, however, would be a very important point to conduct in the future, due to the right amount of fear helping to create more efficacy and precision to the results. Conducting not only haphazardly amounts of fear towards individuals would help to improve research in a massive way. In addition, this thesis suggests that scientists could incorporate a part of qualitatively guided questions as this sheds light on subjective perceptions and attitudes of individuals. This point is important due to every person having a personal and different perspective on the definition offear. If personal differences were taken into account, generalizations could be avoided in future research.

As another implementation drawn from this study, is the necessity to apply the core or the entire nomology of PMT before further non-PMT constructs are added. These conclusions can be drawn by reviewing the studies that Boss conducted (Boss et al. 2015). Many research does not state the value of the PMT in use and why they applied this model. Furthermore, there is no explanation present of why various variables were added and the positive contributions they add to research and findings. Other variables and core elements were eliminated from the research and studies without further explanation. Therefore, the fifth theoretical implication for this research is the better elucidation on why researchers use different models and add or delete different variables. It should be highlighted what contributions those adaptions provide for research. Another point is, that when variables get renamed, there should be a better outlining on the background decisions. Therefore, this thesis proposes common guidelines of the application of using different models. This would be recommendable due to standardization and the resulting comparability of results.

The sixth recommendation of this research is to not only measure behavioral intentions but also to have a look at the actual behavior individuals perform after receiving a threat. In most studies, the actual behaviors of the end users remain unclear (Johnston and Warkentin 2010). In this study, which will be explained in more detail later in the limitation section, only the motivational intentions were explored. The actual behavior of the participants could not be investigated. This is due to the fact that it would not be possible to investigate the short term behaviors to the extent of the duration and length of this thesis. Notwithstanding, this point will be addressed in detail in the limitations.

The last theoretical implementation the study proposes, states not only measure the short-term effects of fear appeals but as well the long-term effects should get outlined. The study by Mwagwabi states the importance in measuring the effects in the ong run (Mwagwabi et al. 2018b). This point is based on the previous one, which states that the current behavior should be measured. When measuring long-term effects it becomes easier to develop personalized and directly tailored to the individual fear appeals afterwards. Also, if the long term effects are more researched, the effects of the fear appeals and the other variables can be, if necessary, adapted to a different extent for future research. If the research does not examine the long term effects, the effectiveness of the investigations may be doubtful.

6.2   Practical Implications

The conceptual framework and the findings that are offered to the reader within this thesis, are recommending several specific and pursuable practical advices for practitioners and for interested parties in this field of research. In this chapter, the thesis is offering also a guideline for further research in practical surroundings. Due to the limitations of this thesis and the study conducted, most of the practical implications are drawn from research and papers reviewed.

The first practical implementation is the provision of instructions or training. These could highlight the current dangers and help individuals to become aware of and improve compliance with password guidelines. One example of this would be sensitization training (Mwagwabi et al. 2018b). This point concerns both sides, the organizational context but can also be applied in the personal context.

In order to give an implication to on the organizational level, the study from Jenkins et al and Menard and his colleagues can be taken into account. They both point out that actions of employees, especially in regard to their personal online accounts, can have serious consequences for companies (Jenkins et al. 2014; Menard et al. 2017). Investigations have demonstrated educational tactics like delivering the facts of the threat to information (Herath and Rao 2009) and making sure end users are responding appropriately (Puhakainen and Siponen 2010) to enhance regulatory security compliance being effective.

In regard to the personal level of protecting assets, proper communication is important, and furthermore it should be precisely designed to align with preventive measures that end users should become encouraged to take. Johnston and his colleague Warketin pointed out that these are well suited, at least in the short term, to entice end users to take more security precautions. Strategies for teaching a course should include demonstrating safety routines that have led to successful outcomes and emphasizing the immediate benefits when the practice is implemented. It is equally beneficial to deploy security skills and assets that enable users to perform security procedures quickly and effectively (Yoon et al. 2012).

Furthermore, personal online accounts such as social networking accounts are at the top of hackers' target lists (Florencio and Herley 2007). Many of these websites contain confidential information such as financial or medical data (Zhang et al. 2009). Manufacturers rely to a large extent on users of these sites themselves to protect their online accounts, e.g. by creating appropriate passwords and changing them regularly. Therefore, an implication in practice is to motivate specific websites to increase their password policies. End users should only be able to set up a user account if they comply with them. Also a regular reminder or request for changing a password on regular basis, could foster security on websites. Those reminders could be directed at the individual directly each quarter.

Another implication of this paper concerns the application of fear appeals. To put them into practice correctly, training, interventions and campaigns are should be provided. The fear arousing communication should be designed to stimulate coping assessment, which in turn leads to an adaptive, protective response instead of a rejection of the message (Herath and Rao 2009).

The last practical implication states that scientists from the field of ISec research should make explored fear appeals, which were applied and approved in science, available accessible to other researchers. Concluding, they can use the same amount of fear arousing communication or customize their message to ensure meaningful results. These outcomes can at the same time be easier compared with results from other studies.

6.3   Limitations and Critical Review of Research

This thesis is designed to offer various extensions and contributions to existing knowledge and research on the topic of privacy online and fear appeal research. Using a quantitative analysis to examine behavioral change incorporating fear appeals based on the PMT model appeared to be beneficial in the context of this study, since the phenomenon has not yet been researched to this extent. Therefore, this thesis is able to give deep insights into the concept and can contribute a lot for further research. Through quantitative examinations it was possible to explore the given context to a very wide extent and to investigate it very deeply due gathering umpteen through the execution of a survey with many respondents. Through the provision of anonymized answers it was possible to get trustworthy and direct answers regarding the topic, which can contribute a significant influence on research. However, the thesis does not claim to be complete and is therefore subject to certain restrictions. Despite emphasizing the benefits of using a quantitative approach, it is to note that this research was subject to strict time regulations, which for example limited the extent of scenario testing within the questionnaire. Reviewing the development and design of the survey, the latter was limited in terms of question types. Using a fixed set of motivation items and excluding open-end questions, limited the possibility to discover aspects that may have not been found during the development process. Though it is to mention, that personal contact existed with a considerate number of respondents after they had completed the survey who expressed their interest in the research objective. Although all people questioned, 284 in total, consisted of 33 different nationalities; Germans were the most represented with a frequency of 68,3% percent. Therefore, generalizability might be given due to missing quantity. For the remaining 32 nationalities only a few people per country participated. Therefore, not that many conclusions can be drawn about the habits of the specific countries. Individuals with another cultural background therefore, might differ in their perspectives as well in their attitudes. It should also be pointed out that, due to the wide age range among respondents and the different professions, there may be large differences in perceptions and related actions for the protection of personal privacy. Since the survey was conducted in two languages and many of the participants are not native English speakers, the language barrier should not be neglected. Furthermore, and as can be stated from the out coming of the data analysis as well, is that a larger amount of participants could be taken into account. Even if different people from several countries have already been questioned, this could be expanded since most of them were in the same age as the researcher.

Further limitations regarding the questionnaire and the associated data collected may have been indicated in subchapter 4.7 including the unavailability of data on canceled questionnaires.

Another important limitation to the present work is that the survey only examined intentions regarding behavioral changes and not the actual attitude differences. At the beginning, the study also aimed to investigate the former, but it turned out to be very difficult to implement in practice, since not all participants of the study could be identified, due to carrying out the study anonymously. Before designing the study, it was considered to contact all participants again two weeks after participating in the study and to ask whether the password of the e-mail address had now been changed or not. However, this turned out to be difficult, as not every single respondent could be identified afterwards. The link to the survey was posted on various forums and so it was not possible to identify the individual participants or would have required a larger time frame for the thesis. However, the researcher received feedback from several study participants shortly after the study that they changed their passwords after the study.

Another important limitation of this thesis is, that only the short term effects could be investigated and therefore were in the focus of the research conducted. What influence the fear appeal now has in the long run cannot be taken into account in this research and should definitely be included in further research. It should be added that changes could also arise, particularly in the long term, as a result of the new data protection regulation. The thesis was written at the time the new data protection regulation was issued, but after the survey was carried out. It is therefore possible that, as a result of the expanding focus on data protection, the general caution of the population regarding their personal data security will raise in the future. In addition, the ever-increasing security concerns could lead to a loss of security. Furthermore, it could become generally more difficult for hackers to steal data due to the enlarging security barriers.

The literature analysis for the theoretical background was implemented with involving the most prestigious Journals of Information Systems as well as relevant literature within books or new current emerging topics from trustworthy internet sources. Although these methods certainly include a large part of the relevant scientific literature, it cannot guaranteed a complete coverage in the examined field of research. Regarding the search within the Journals, pre-set search terms were used to find relevant literature and there is a possibility that existing literature was not identified and thus, has not been recorded into the revision. Furthermore, solely one author was in charge for conducting the research and elaborating the paper and hence, a general objectivity cannot be assured.

Participants in the survey were selected randomly dependent from disposability as described above and their willingness to be part of the research and therefore, limits the generalizability. Due to the fact that only a single application of fear appeals as well one single context, data leaks, were used, this may not have been sufficient to test the effects of fear appeals on an adequate dimension and could therefore be counted as another limitation of this study. Further research needs to continue to investigate other contexts in order to correctly identify the effectiveness of research based on PMT and propose further improvements in this area

This thesis offered new insights for advantages for the usage of the fear appeals using the PMT as a basis in order to measure behavioral changes of individuals on the topic of privacy. It would be from enormous interest to examine more motivational factors and impacts as well as personal opinions of fear appeals and their effects with carrying out a qualitative analysis. Those personal experiences and assessments could contribute a lot to researcher and also help improving some practical approaches.

7.   Conclusion

In the beginning of this paper, lack in fear appeal research in the field of ISec research has been introduced - predominantly based on reviewing research conducted. The gap in literature, offered little to no ground for understanding the impact of fear appeals behind a change in protection motivation. Moreover, no existing data on the scope of this segment existed which provided reasons to assume that it may be a neglectable niche that may not require in-depth research. The objectives of this study were therefore defined as to not only explore and examine the if users would seek to improve their protection if they were aware of their lack of privacy online motivation behind the intention to protect personal assets online but also to provide findings that will support the justification and significance of conducting research on this phenomenon with adding fear appeals more specifically tailored various studies. This paper specifically aimed at identifying the impact of fear appeals building the motivation behind protection intentional constructs, by using the PMT model as a basis. In more general terms, it aimed at making a valuable contribution to the field of research in the field of information systems. The research process included primary data sources from a survey specially designed and conducted for this thesis resulting in two independent data sets, a group exposed to fear appeals and one not confronted with fear appeals. The data of both groups delivered significant insights to the phenomenon under research. Results included not only the desired profound knowledge about the composition of the fear appeal construct but also meaningful information about the impact on fear appeals on the remaining variables of the protection motivation theory.

As stated in Chapter 2, digitalization creates outstanding problems online for end users, including their deficient of privacy online. Although most people are aware of these problems, many end users are still far too careless with their data. Many hackers and unauthorized third parties obtain data from individuals.

In order to answer the research question of this thesis, if people reconsider their behavior when they are informed that their data, such as passwords or e-mail addresses, are accessible on the internet, a questionnaire was designed and could be filled out online.

This survey built the core of this paper while it got adapted from the PMT model which was presented former in the thesis und built the basis for the survey.

The survey was conducted by 284 persons by which 214 data sheets could be used due to the completion of the entire survey. Out of the participants 169 were female (59,5%) and 96 were male (33,8%). The language the survey was filled out was German for 217 people (76,4 %) and 67 respondents took answered the questionnaire in English (23,6%). The sample consisted of 33 different nationalities which German being the most often nationality with 194 of the respondents (68,3%). Out of the respondents, 100 people, which adds up to 35,2%, stated that there is a data leak on one of their online user accounts according to the website. 125 (44 %) stated, there was no data leak in their online user accounts. 59 respondents (20,8%) did not give a response.

The motivational intention construct of the people surveyed, was explored in a one-step process. A set of 32 questions was developed consulting secondary data sources of former ISec research and with the usage of PMT and academic literature and prompted within the scope of an online questionnaire. Respondents were asked to rate the items, every dimension of the PMT research got at least three questions, respectively to their level of agreement on a 7-point Likert scale. The evaluation of the data by SPSS, by carrying out a multiple linear regression, showed that there is, for both groups, a positive correlation between the variables perceived threat severity on fear and fear on protection motivation. Self-efficacy and response costs showed also significant effects on protection motivation but were only stated for the group without fear appeals. The rest of the PMT model did not hold, due to a too low application of fear arousing communication posed at the individuals. Therefore, the research question can be answered by stating, that people indeed do reconsider their behavioral intentions when they were informed that private information, such as passwords or e-mail addresses, were accessible on the internet.

Based on the summary of key findings of this study, the author concludes that the initial objectives of this research were met. Valuable insights were presented in order to gain a profound understanding of the impact of fear appeals on protection motivation of individuals in display on the protection of their personal assets online. With reference to the introductory statement of Edward Snowden, results of this study stress the importance of primarily understanding the importance of the protection and severity of not assuring personal privacy compliance online. Given the profound knowledge gained on both aspects, providing implications regarding the contribution of fear appeal research were facilitated.

References

"2018 Reform of EU Data Protection Rules." 2018. *European Commission - European Commission*, , May. (https://ec.europa.eu/commission/priorities/justice-and-fundamental-rights/data-protection/2018-reform-eu-data-protection-rules_en, accessed August 3, 2018).

Adams, A., and Sasse, M. A. 1999. "Users Are Not the Enemy," *Communications of the ACM* (42:12), pp. 40–46. (https://doi.org/10.1145/322796.322806).

Alashoor, T., Aryal, A., and Kenny, G. (n.d.). "Understanding the Privacy Issue in the Digital Age: An Expert Perspective," *Emergent Research Forum Papers*, p. 5.

Albers, S. (ed.). 2009. *Methodik der empirischen Forschung*, (3., überarb. und erw. Aufl.), Wiesbaden: Gabler.

Alqahtani, F., Watson, J., and Partridge, H. 2014. "Organizational Support and Enterprise Web 2.0 Adoption: A Qualitative Study," *Twentieth Americas Conference on Information Systems, Savannah, 2014*, p. 9.

Alsunbul, S. A., Le, P. D., Newmarch, J., and Tan, J. 2016. "A Dynamic Security Model for Addressing Hacking Risk Factors," *INTERNATIONAL CONFERENCE ON INFORMATION SYSTEMS DEVELOPMENT* ((ISD2016 POLAND)), p. 9.

Angst, and Agarwal. 2009. "Adoption of Electronic Health Records in the Presence of Privacy Concerns: The Elaboration Likelihood Model and Individual Persuasion," *MIS Quarterly* (33:2), p. 339. (https://doi.org/10.2307/20650295).

Awad, and Krishnan. 2006. "The Personalization Privacy Paradox: An Empirical Evaluation of Information Transparency and the Willingness to Be Profiled Online for Personalization," *MIS Quarterly* (30:1), p. 13. (https://doi.org/10.2307/25148715).

Baur, N., and Fromm, S. 2008. *Datenanalyse mit SPSS für Fortgeschrittene Ein Arbeitsbuch*, Wiesbaden: VS Verlag für Sozialwissenschaften / GWV Fachverlage GmbH, Wiesbaden. (http://dx.doi.org/10.1007/978-3-531-91034-5).

Beautement, A., Sasse, M. A., and Wonham, M. 2008. *The Compliance Budget: Managing Security Behaviour in Organisations*, ACM Press, p. 47. (https://doi.org/10.1145/1595676.1595684).

Bélanger, and Crossler. 2011. "Privacy in the Digital Age: A Review of Information Privacy Research in Information Systems," *MIS Quarterly* (35:4), p. 1017. (https://doi.org/10.2307/41409971).

Bonneau, J., and Preibusch, S. 2010. "The Password Thicket: Technical and Market Failures in Human Authentication on the Web," *WEIS 2010 The Ninth Workshop on the Economics of Information Security*, p. 48.

Boss, S. R., University of Pittsburgh, Lowry, P. B., City University of Hong Kong, Moody, G. D., University of Nevada, Las Vegas, Polak, P., and Florida International University. 2015. "What Do Systems Users Have to Fear? Using Fear Appeals to Engender Threats and Fear That Motivate Protective Security Behaviors," *MIS Quarterly* (39:4), pp. 837–864. (https://doi.org/10.25300/MISQ/2015/39.4.5).

Bradberry, C., and Nemati, H. 2014. "Privacy Momentum: A New Contextually Dynamic

Conceptualization of Privacy," *Twentieth Americas Conference on Information Systems, Savannah, 2014*, p. 7.

Brosius, F. 2011. *SPSS 19*, (1. Aufl.), Heidelberg: Mitp.

Brosius, F. 2013. *SPSS 21: fundierte Einführung in SPSS und in die Statistik; alle statistischen Verfahren mit praxisnahen Beispielen; inklusive CD-ROM*, (1. Aufl.), Heidelberg Hamburg: Mitp, Verl.-Gruppe Hüthig, Jehle, Rehm.

Bulgurcu, Cavusoglu, and Benbasat. 2010. "Information Security Policy Compliance: An Empirical Study of Rationality-Based Beliefs and Information Security Awareness," *MIS Quarterly* (34:3), p. 523. (https://doi.org/10.2307/25750690).

Burzan, N. 2015. *Quantitative Methoden kompakt*, UTB Sozialwissenschaften, Kultur- und Kommunikationswissenschaft, Konstanz: UVK Verlagsgesellschaft mbH.

Carstens, D. S., McCauley-Bell, P. R., Malone, L. C., and DeMara, R. F. 2004. "Evaluation of the Human Impact of Password Authentication Practices on Information Security," *Informing Science Journal*, p. 19.

Chen, Y. 2017. "Examining Internet Users' Adaptive and Maladaptive Security Behaviors Using the Extended Parallel Process Model," *ICIS 2017 Proceedings*, p. 14.

Cheng, L., Liu, F., and Yao, D. D. 2017. "Enterprise Data Breach: Causes, Challenges, Prevention, and Future Directions: Enterprise Data Breach," *Wiley Interdisciplinary Reviews: Data Mining and Knowledge Discovery* (7:5), p. e1211. (https://doi.org/10.1002/widm.1211).

Claar, C. L., and Johnson, J. 2012. "ANALYZING HOME PC SECURITY ADOPTION BEHAVIOR," *Journal of Computer Information Systems*, p. 10.

Cole, D., Nelson, J., and McDaniel, B. 2015. "Benefits and Risks of Big Data," *Association for Information Systems AIS Electronic Library (AISeL)* (SAIS 2015 Proceedings), p. 6.

"Commission Staff Working Paper Impact Assessment /* SEC/2012/0072 Final */." 2018. *EUR-Lex; Access to European Union Law*, , May. (https://eur-lex.europa.eu/legal-content/EN/TXT/?uri=celex:52012SC0072, accessed August 3, 2018).

"Conferences - Association for Information Systems (AIS)." 2018. (https://aisnet.org/page/ICISPage, accessed July 27, 2018).

"Cost of Data Breach Study | IBM Security." 2018. *IBM*. (https://www.ibm.com/security/data-breach, accessed April 4, 2018).

Crossler, R., and Bélanger, F. 2014. "An Extended Perspective on Individual Security Behaviors: Protection Motivation Theory and a Unified Security Practices (USP) Instrument," *ACM SIGMIS Database* (45:4), pp. 51–71. (https://doi.org/10.1145/2691517.2691521).

Crossler, R. E. 2010. "Protection Motivation Theory: Understanding Determinants to Backing Up Personal Data," *Proceedings of the 43rd Hawaii International Conference on System Sciences*. (https://www.computer.org/csdl/proceedings/hicss/2010/3869/00/07-03-04.pdf).

Crossler, R. E., Long, J. H., Loraas, T. M., and Trinkle, B. S. 2014. "Understanding Compliance with Bring Your Own Device Policies Utilizing Protection Motivation Theory:

Bridging the Intention-Behavior Gap," *Journal of Information Systems* (28:1), pp. 209–226. (https://doi.org/10.2308/isys-50704).

Culnan, M. J. 1993. "'How Did They Get My Name?': An Exploratory Investigation of Consumer Attitudes toward Secondary Information Use," *MIS Quarterly* (17:3), p. 341. (https://doi.org/10.2307/249775).

Culnan, M. J., and Armstrong, P. K. 1999. "Information Privacy Concerns, Procedural Fairness, and Impersonal Trust: An Empirical Investigation," *Organization Science* (10:1), pp. 104–115. (https://doi.org/10.1287/orsc.10.1.104).

Das, A., Bonneau, J., Caesar, M., Borisov, N., and Wang, X. 2014. *The Tangled Web of Password Reuse*, presented at the NDSS Symposium 2014, Internet Society. (https://doi.org/10.14722/ndss.2014.23357).

Dutta, A., and Roy, R. (n.d.). *The Dynamics of Organizational Information Security*, p. 8.

Eckstein, P. P. 2016. *Angewandte Statistik mit SPSS*, Wiesbaden: Springer Fachmedien Wiesbaden. (https://doi.org/10.1007/978-3-658-10918-9).

European Commission. 2018. *A New Era for Data Protection in the EU - What Changes after May 2018*. (https://ec.europa.eu/commission/sites/beta-political/files/data-protection-factsheet-changes_en.pdf).

Florencio, D., and Herley, C. 2007. *A Large-Scale Study of Web Password Habits*, ACM Press, p. 657. (https://doi.org/10.1145/1242572.1242661).

Galanxhi, H., and Nah, F. F. 2006. "Privacy Issues in the Era of Ubiquitous Commerce," *Electronic Markets* (16:3), pp. 222–232. (https://doi.org/10.1080/10196780600841894).

Gochman, D. S. (ed.). 1997. *Handbook of Health Behavior Research*, New York: Plenum Press.

Grossklags, J., and Acquisti, A. 2007. *When 25 Cents Is Too Much: An Experiment on Willingness-To-Sell and Willingness-To-Protect Personal Information*, p. 22.

Habryn, F., and Kunze, J. 2012. "A BUSINESS INTELLIGENCE SOLUTION FOR ASSESSING CUSTOMER INTERACTION, CROSS-SELLING, AND CUSTOMIZATION IN A CUSTOMER INTIMACY CONTEXT," *ECIS 2012 Proceedings*, p. 13.

Han, C. C. (n.d.). *THE FEAR MANAGEMENT MODEL: BUILDING AN INTEGRATIVE FEAR APPEAL THEORY THROUGH SYSTEM DYNAMICS*, p. 27.

Harrington, S., Anderson, C., and Agarwal, R. 2006. "Practicing Safe Computing: Message Framing, Self-View, and Home Computer User Security Behavior Intentions," *ICIS 2006 Proceedings International Conference on Information Systems*, p. 21.

Hatzinger, R., and Nagel, H. 2009. *PASW Statistics: statistische Methoden und Fallbeispiele ; [ehemals SPSS]*, st - scientific tools, München: Pearson Studium.

"Have I Been Pwned? Who, What & Why." (n.d.). (https://haveibeenpwned.com/About, accessed March 24, 2018).

Herath, T., Chen, R., Wang, J., Banjara, K., Wilbur, J., and Rao, H. R. 2012. "Security Services as Coping Mechanisms: An Investigation into User Intention to Adopt an Email

Authentication Service: Security Services as Coping Mechanisms," *Information Systems Journal* (24:1), pp. 61–84. (https://doi.org/10.1111/j.1365-2575.2012.00420.x).

Herath, T., and Rao, H. R. 2009. "Protection Motivation and Deterrence: A Framework for Security Policy Compliance in Organisations," *European Journal of Information Systems* (18:2), pp. 106–125. (https://doi.org/10.1057/ejis.2009.6).

Herley, C., and Van Oorschot, P. 2012. "A Research Agenda Acknowledging the Persistence of Passwords," *IEEE Security & Privacy Magazine* (10:1), pp. 28–36. (https://doi.org/10.1109/MSP.2011.150).

Herr, C. 2007. *Nicht-lineare Wirkungsbeziehungen von Erfolgsfaktoren der Unternehmensgründung*, (1. Aufl.), Gabler Edition Wissenschaft Entrepreneurship, Wiesbaden: Dt. Univ.-Verl.

de Hoog, N., Stroebe, W., and de Wit, J. B. F. 2008. "The Processing of Fear-arousing Communications: How Biased Processing Leads to Persuasion," *Social Influence* (3:2), pp. 84–113. (https://doi.org/10.1080/15534510802185836).

Hunt, T. 2018. "The UK and Australian Governments Are Now Monitoring Their Gov Domains on Have I Been Pwned," *Troy Hunt*, , March 1. (https://www.troyhunt.com/the-uk-and-australian-governments-are-now-monitoring-their-gov-domains-on-have-i-been-pwned/, accessed August 11, 2018).

Huth, A., Orlando, M., and Pesante, L. 2012. *Password Security, Protection, and Management*, p. 5.

Ifinedo, P. 2012. "Understanding Information Systems Security Policy Compliance: An Integration of the Theory of Planned Behavior and the Protection Motivation Theory," *Computers & Security* (31:1), pp. 83–95. (https://doi.org/10.1016/j.cose.2011.10.007).

Im, G. P., and Baskerville, R. L. 2005. "A Longitudinal Study of Information System Threat Categories: The Enduring Problem of Human Error," *ACM SIGMIS Database: The DATABASE for Advances in Information Systems* (36:4), pp. 68–79. (https://doi.org/10.1145/1104004.1104010).

Jannsen, J., and Laatz, W. 1999. *Statistische Datenanalyse mit SPSS für Windows Eine anwendungsorientierte Einführung in das Basissystem Version 8 und das Modul Exakte Tests*, Berlin, Heidelberg: Springer Berlin Heidelberg. (http://nbn-resolving.de/urn:nbn:de:1111-201304112912).

Jenkins, J. L., Grimes, M., Proudfoot, J. G., and Lowry, P. B. 2014. "Improving Password Cybersecurity Through Inexpensive and Minimally Invasive Means: Detecting and Deterring Password Reuse Through Keystroke-Dynamics Monitoring and Just-in-Time Fear Appeals," *Information Technology for Development* (20:2), pp. 196–213. (https://doi.org/10.1080/02681102.2013.814040).

Johnston, A. C., Mississippi State University, Siponen, M., and University of Jyväskylä. 2015. "An Enhanced Fear Appeal Rhetorical Framework: Leveraging Threats to the Human Asset Through Sanctioning Rhetoric," *MIS Quarterly* (39:1), pp. 113–134. (https://doi.org/10.25300/MISQ/2015/39.1.06).

Johnston, A. C., and Siponen, M. 2015. "An Enhanced Fear Appeal Rhetorical Framework: Leveraging Threats to the Human Asset Through Sanctioning Rhetoric," *MIS Quarterly* (39:1), pp. 113–134. (https://doi.org/10.25300/MISQ/2015/39.1.06).

Johnston, and Warkentin. 2010. "Fear Appeals and Information Security Behaviors: An Empirical Study," *MIS Quarterly* (34:3), p. 549. (https://doi.org/10.2307/25750691).

Kaul, T. 2014. *Multiple lineare Regression & High Performance Computing Methodik und Software-Implementation komplexer Analysemodelle*, Norderstedt: Books on Demand. (http://nbn-resolving.de/urn:nbn:de:101:1-2014122506).

Krentz, H. 2009. *Grafische Darstellung statistischer Kennwerte*, Statistische Analysen mit SPSS in der Medizin, Aachen: Shaker.

Kshetri, N. 2014. "Big Data's Impact on Privacy, Security and Consumer Welfare," *Telecommunications Policy* (38:11), pp. 1134–1145. (https://doi.org/10.1016/j.telpol.2014.10.002).

Lai, F., Li, D., and Hsieh, C.-T. 2012. "Fighting Identity Theft: The Coping Perspective," *Decision Support Systems* (52:2), pp. 353–363. (https://doi.org/10.1016/j.dss.2011.09.002).

LaRose, R., Rifon, N. J., and Enbody, R. 2008. "Promoting Personal Responsibility for Internet Safety," *Communications of the ACM* (51:3), pp. 71–76. (https://doi.org/10.1145/1325555.1325569).

Lee, D., Larose, R., and Rifon, N. 2008. "Keeping Our Network Safe: A Model of Online Protection Behaviour," *Behaviour & Information Technology* (27:5), pp. 445–454. (https://doi.org/10.1080/01449290600879344).

Lee, Y. 2011. "Understanding Anti-Plagiarism Software Adoption: An Extended Protection Motivation Theory Perspective," *Decision Support Systems* (50:2), pp. 361–369. (https://doi.org/10.1016/j.dss.2010.07.009).

Lee, Y., and Larsen, K. R. 2009. "Threat or Coping Appraisal: Determinants of SMB Executives' Decision to Adopt Anti-Malware Software," *European Journal of Information Systems* (18:2), pp. 177–187. (https://doi.org/10.1057/ejis.2009.11).

Leventhal, H. 1970. "Findings and Theory in the Study of Fear Communications," in *Advances in Experimental Social Psychology* (Vol. 5), Elsevier, pp. 119–186. (https://doi.org/10.1016/S0065-2601(08)60091-X).

Liang, H., and Xue, Y. 2010. "Understanding Security Behaviors in Personal Computer Usage: A Threat Avoidance Perspective," *Journal of the Association for Information Systems* (11:07), pp. 394–413. (https://doi.org/10.17705/1jais.00232).

Mai, B., Menon, N. M., and Sarkar, S. 2010. "No Free Lunch: Price Premium for Privacy Seal-Bearing Vendors," *Journal of Management Information Systems* (27:2), pp. 189–212. (https://doi.org/10.2753/MIS0742-1222270206).

Mai, J.-E. 2016. "Big Data Privacy: The Datafication of Personal Information," *The Information Society* (32:3), pp. 192–199. (https://doi.org/10.1080/01972243.2016.1153010).

Marett, K., Niagara University, and Harris, R. 2011. "Social Networking Websites and Posting Personal Information: An Evaluation of Protection Motivation Theory," *AIS Transactions on Human-Computer Interaction* (3:3), pp. 170–188. (https://doi.org/10.17705/1thci.00032).

McLoughlin, C., and Lee, M. J. W. 2007. "Social Software and Participatory Learning:

Pedagogical Choices with Technology Affordances in the Web 2.0 Era," *Proceedings Ascilite Singapore 2007*, p. 12.

Menard, P., Bott, G. J., and Crossler, R. E. 2017. "User Motivations in Protecting Information Security: Protection Motivation Theory Versus Self-Determination Theory," *Journal of Management Information Systems* (34:4), pp. 1203–1230. (https://doi.org/10.1080/07421222.2017.1394083).

Miller, and Zumbansen. 2005. *Review of Developments in German, European and International Jurisprudence*, GERMAN LAW JOURNAL. (https://static1.squarespace.com/static/56330ad3e4b0733dcc0c8495/t/5763466137c5 818b48e4fd8c/1466123875942/GLJ_vol_06_no_07.pdf).

Mwagwabi, F., McGill, T., and Dixon, M. 2018a. "Short-Term and Long-Term Effects of Fear Appeals in Improving Compliance with Password Guidelines," *Communications of the Association for Information Systems* (42). (https://doi.org/10.17705/1CAIS.04207).

Mwagwabi, F., McGill, T., and Dixon, M. 2018b. "Short-Term and Long-Term Effects of Fear Appeals in Improving Compliance with Password Guidelines," *Communications of the Association for Information Systems* (42). (https://doi.org/10.17705/1CAIS.04207).

Mylonas, A., Kastania, A., and Gritzalis, D. 2013. "Delegate the Smartphone User? Security Awareness in Smartphone Platforms," *Computers & Security* (34), pp. 47–66. (https://doi.org/10.1016/j.cose.2012.11.004).

Ng, B.-Y., Kankanhalli, A., and Xu, Y. (Calvin). 2009. "Studying Users' Computer Security Behavior: A Health Belief Perspective," *Decision Support Systems* (46:4), pp. 815–825. (https://doi.org/10.1016/j.dss.2008.11.010).

Phelps, J., Nowak, G., and Ferrell, E. 2000. "Privacy Concerns and Consumer Willingness to Provide Personal Information," *Journal of Public Policy & Marketing* (19:1), pp. 27–41. (https://doi.org/10.1509/jppm.19.1.27.16941).

Pitta, D. A., Franzak, F., and Laric, M. 2003. "Privacy and One-to-one Marketing: Resolving the Conflict," *Journal of Consumer Marketing* (20:7), pp. 616–628. (https://doi.org/10.1108/07363760310506157).

Popova, L. 2012. "The Extended Parallel Process Model: Illuminating the Gaps in Research," *Health Education & Behavior* (39:4), pp. 455–473. (https://doi.org/10.1177/1090198111418108).

Posey, C., Roberts, T. L., and Lowry, P. B. 2015. "The Impact of Organizational Commitment on Insiders' Motivation to Protect Organizational Information Assets," *Journal of Management Information Systems* (32:4), pp. 179–214. (https://doi.org/10.1080/07421222.2015.1138374).

Puhakainen, and Siponen. 2010. "Improving Employees' Compliance Through Information Systems Security Training: An Action Research Study," *MIS Quarterly* (34:4), p. 757. (https://doi.org/10.2307/25750704).

"Pwned | Define Pwned at Dictionary.Com." 2018. (http://www.dictionary.com/browse/pwned, accessed March 24, 2018).

Ranganathan, and Grandon. 2002. *An Exploratory Examination of Factors Affecting Online Sales*, p. 8.

Regan. 1995. *Legislating Privacy: Technology, Social Values and Public Policy*, Chapel Hill: The University of North Carolina Press. (https://ojs.library.dal.ca/djls/article/view-File/5573/5018.).

"Regulation (EU) 2016/679 of the European Parliament and of the Council of 27 April 2016." 2016. *OJ L* (Vol. 119). (http://data.europa.eu/eli/reg/2016/679/oj/eng).

Rogers, R. W. 1975. "A Protection Motivation Theory of Fear Appeals and Attitude Change1," *The Journal of Psychology* (91:1), pp. 93–114. (https://doi.org/10.1080/00223980.1975.9915803).

Romero, A. D. 2015. "Mass E-Mail Surveillance: The next Battle," *Sur - International Journal on Human Rights*, , August 20. (http://sur.conectas.org/en/the-next-battle-an-internet-human-rights-movement/, accessed August 4, 2018).

Roskos-Ewoldsen, D. R., Yu, J. H., and Rhodes, N. 2004. "Fear Appeal Messages Affect Accessibility of Attitudes toward the Threat and Adaptive Behaviors," *Communication Monographs* (71:1), pp. 49–69. (https://doi.org/10.1080/0363452042000228559).

Schuchmann, M. 2016. *Einstieg in die Datenanalyse mit SPSS*. (http://nbn-resolving.de/urn:nbn:de:101:1-2016061715206).

Schwartz, E. 2016. "Zum Jahresausklang: Die 3 Wichtigsten Tipps Für Umfragen 2016," *SurveyMonkey Germany*, , December 8. (https://de.surveymonkey.com/blog/de/2016/12/08/jahresausklang-3-top-umfragetipps-2016/, accessed August 5, 2018).

Seligman, M. E. P., and Csikszentmihalyi, M. 2000. "Positive Psychology: An Introduction.," *American Psychologist* (55:1), pp. 5–14. (https://doi.org/10.1037/0003-066X.55.1.5).

Shevlyakov, G. L., and Oja, H. 2016. *Robust Correlation: Theory and Applications*, Wiley Series in Probability and Statistics, Chichester, West Sussex: Wiley.

Siponen, M., Pahnila, S., and Mahmood, M. A. 2010. "Compliance with Information Security Policies: An Empirical Investigation," *Computer* (43:2), pp. 64–71. (https://doi.org/10.1109/MC.2010.35).

Siponen, M. T., and Oinas-Kukkonen, H. 2007. "A Review of Information Security Issues and Respective Research Contributions," *ACM SIGMIS Database* (38:1), p. 60. (https://doi.org/10.1145/1216218.1216224).

Smith, H. J., Milberg, S. J., and Burke, S. J. 1996. "Information Privacy: Measuring Individuals' Concerns about Organizational Practices," *MIS Quarterly* (20:2), p. 167. (https://doi.org/10.2307/249477).

von Solms, R., and van Niekerk, J. 2013. "From Information Security to Cyber Security," *Computers & Security* (38), pp. 97–102. (https://doi.org/10.1016/j.cose.2013.04.004).

Stephen, A. T. 2016. "The Role of Digital and Social Media Marketing in Consumer Behavior," *Current Opinion in Psychology* (10), pp. 17–21. (https://doi.org/10.1016/j.copsyc.2015.10.016).

"Timehop Data Breach: Millions of Users in Europe Compromised." 2018. *The Telegraph*, , July 11. (https://www.telegraph.co.uk/technology/2018/07/11/timehop-data-breach-millions-users-europe-compromised/, accessed August 3, 2018).

Ur, B., Kelley, P. G., Komanduri, S., Lee, J., Maass, M., Mazurek, M. L., Passaro, T., Shay, R., Vidas, T., Bauer, L., Christin, N., and Cranor, L. F. 2012. "How Does Your Password Measure Up? The Effect of Strength Meters on Password Creation," *21 St Usenix Security Symposium*, p. 16.

Van Dyke, T., Midha, V., and Nemati, H. 2007. "The Effect of Consumer Privacy Empowerment on Trust and Privacy Concerns in E-Commerce," *Electronic Markets* (17:1), pp. 68–81. (https://doi.org/10.1080/10196780601136997).

Vance, A., Eargle, D., Ouimet, K., and Straub, D. 2013. *Enhancing Password Security through Interactive Fear Appeals: A Web-Based Field Experiment*, IEEE, January, pp. 2988–2997. (https://doi.org/10.1109/HICSS.2013.196).

Wall, J. D., and Buche, M. W. 2017. "To Fear or Not to Fear? A Critical Review and Analysis of Fear Appeals in the Information Security Context," *Communications of the Association for Information Systems* (41), p. 25.

Web Application Security Consortium: Threat Classification. 2004. Web Application Security Consortium.

Webster, J., and Watson, R. T. 2002. "Guest Editorial: Analyzing the Past to Prepare for the Future: Writing a Literature Review," *Management Information Systems Research Center*, p. 11.

Westin, A. F. 1968. *Privacy And Freedom*, p. 6.

Westin, A. F. 2003. "Social and Political Dimensions of Privacy," *Journal of Social Issues* (59:2), pp. 431–453. (https://doi.org/10.1111/1540-4560.00072).

Witte, K. 1992. "Putting the Fear Back into Fear Appeals: The Extended Parallel Process Model," *Communication Monographs* (59:4), pp. 329–349. (https://doi.org/10.1080/03637759209376276).

Witte, K. 1994. "Fear Control and Danger Control: A Test of the Extended Parallel Process Model (EPPM)," *Communication Monographs* (61:2), pp. 113–134. (https://doi.org/10.1080/03637759409376328).

Woon, I. M. Y., Tan, G. W., and Low, R. T. 2015. "A Protection Motivation Theory Approach to Home Wireless Security," *Twenty-Sixth International Conference on Information Systems*, p. 14.

Workman, M., Bommer, W. H., and Straub, D. 2008. "Security Lapses and the Omission of Information Security Measures: A Threat Control Model and Empirical Test," *Computers in Human Behavior* (24:6), pp. 2799–2816. (https://doi.org/10.1016/j.chb.2008.04.005).

Yao, M. Z., Rice, R. E., and Wallis, K. 2007. "Predicting User Concerns about Online Privacy," *Journal of the American Society for Information Science and Technology* (58:5), pp. 710–722. (https://doi.org/10.1002/asi.20530).

Yoon, C., Hwang, J.-W., and Kim, R. 2012. "Exploring Factors That Influence Students' Behaviors in Information Security," *Journal of Information Systems Education, Vol. 23(4) Winter 2012* (23), p. 10.

Zhang, L., and McDowell, W. 2009. *Modeling Online Passwords Protection Intention*, p. 10.

Zhang, L., Smith, W. W., and McDowell, W. C. 2009. "Examining Digital Piracy: Self-Control, Punishment, and Self-Efficacy," *Information Resources Management Journal* (22:1), pp. 24–44. (https://doi.org/10.4018/irmj.2009010102).

Appendix

A. Survey Data Leaks and Password Security – English Version

Survey data leaks and password security

Dear participant,

thank you for taking part in the survey on "Data protection behaviour of private end users on the Internet ".

The focus of this survey is to determine whether your online user accounts (e.g. e-mail, LinkedIn, Dropbox, etc.) and related personal data are at risk from data protection violations. At the beginning of the survey you will be redirected to a page asking you to have your online accounts checked for data leaks.

After checking your data you will be asked to answer a few questions on this topic.

You can find an information video about the website here (https://videos.chip.de/p/1741931/sp/174193100/serveFlavor/entryid/1_2z34drrm/v/1/flavorId/1_0ohixzj0/name/a.mp4)

This survey is part of my master thesis at the Chair of Information Systems in Services, at the University of Bamberg. The participation is anonymous, so that no conclusions about your person are possible.

Many thanks in advance

There are 10 questions in this survey

General information
[]Gender
Please choose only one of the following:

○ Female
○ Male

[]Age
Only numbers may be entered in this field.

Please write your answer here:

[   ]

[]Nationality
Please write your answer here:

[   ]

[]Highest level of education

Choose one of the following answers:

Please choose only one of the following:

○ High School Diploma
○ Associate Degree
○ Apprenticeship
○ Bachelor's degree
○ Master's degree
○ Diploma
○ Other

[]Current professional status

Choose one of the following answers

Please choose only one of the following:

○ Pupil
○ Student
○ Apprentice/r
○ Employee
○ Self-employed
○ Other

Test data leaks in online user accounts

Under the following **link** you will find the website mentioned above which tests your online user accounts for potential data leaks based on your e-mail address. A data leak is an incident in which unauthorized parties gain insight into the collection of data.

https://haveibeenpwned.com (https://haveibeenpwned.com)

Please enter your e-mail address in the empty line & press "pwned?".

Please use the email address you use most often for your online accounts.

If there is no data leak, you will see the following:

If there is at least one data leak, the following display appears.

If you see the latter, scroll down to see which of your online user accounts is affected.

After completing the test, please return to this survey and answer the remaining questions.

[]Is there a data leak on one of your online user accounts according to the website?

Choose one of the following answers

Please choose only one of the following:

○ yes
○ no

[]Is the email address you checked your main e-mail address?

Choose one of the following answers

Please choose only one of the following:

○ yes
○ no

data leaks in online user accounts

[]Assessing the relevance and timeliness of data leaks in private user accounts

Please choose the appropriate response for each item.

	Strongly disagree	Disagree	Somewhat disagree	Neither agree nor disagree	Somewhat agree	Agree	Strongly agree
A potential data leak could occur with one of my online user accounts.	O	O	O	O	O	O	O
With one of my online user accounts a potential data leak would be serious.	O	O	O	O	O	O	O
With one of my online user accounts, a potential data leak would have significant consequences.	O	O	O	O	O	O	O
There is a possibility that personal information may be disclosed through a data leak in one of my online user accounts.	O	O	O	O	O	O	O
There is a possibility that personal information may be affected in the future by disclosure due to a data leak.	O	O	O	O	O	O	O
It is unlikely that I will lose data in the future due to a data leak in one of my online user	O	O	O	O	O	O	O

	Strongly disagree	Disagree	Somewhat disagree	Neither agree nor disagree	Somewhat agree	Agree	Strongly agree
accounts. It is more time-saving not to change the passwords of my online user accounts.	O	O	O	O	O	O	O
It is more money-saving not to change the passwords of my online user accounts.	O	O	O	O	O	O	O
The constant change of passwords in my online user accounts confuses me	O	O	O	O	O,	O	O,

data leaks in online user accounts

[]
Assessing the relevance and timeliness of data leaks in private user accounts

Please choose the appropriate response for each item.

	Strongly disagree	Disagree	Somewhat disagree	Neither agree nor disagree	Somewhat agree	Agree	Strongly agree
Due to the constant change of passwords, there is a risk of forgetting the current password.	O	O	O	O	O	O	O
Permanent password changes are an effective protection against data theft on one	O	O	O	O	O	O	O

	Strongly disagree	Disagree	Somewhat disagree	Neither agree nor disagree	Somewhat agree	Agree	Strongly agree
...of my online user accounts.	○	○	○	○	○	○	○
Permanent password changes are a good way to protect my data from data theft on one of my online user accounts.	○	○	○	○	○	○	○
By permanently changing passwords I would reduce the possibility of data theft on one of my online user accounts.	○	○	○	○	○	○	○
I am able to protect my personal user accounts from data theft.	○	○	○	○	○	○	○
Protecting my personal user accounts from data theft is a big effort for me.	○	○	○	○	○	○	○
I feel comfortable taking measures to increase the security of my online user accounts.	○	○	○	○	○	○	○
Changing passwords regularly would require too much time.	○	○	○	○	○	○	○

data leaks in online user accounts

[ ]Assessing the relevance and timeliness of data leaks in private user accounts

Please choose the appropriate response for each item.

	Strongly disagree	Disagree	Somewhat disagree	Neither agree nor disagree	Somewhat agree	Agree	Strongly agree
The cost of regularly changing the password reduces the convenience of the application.	○	○	○	○	○	○	○
I do not attach great importance to the regular change of my passwords.	○	○	○	○	○	○	○
Potential data leaks are alarming.	○	○	○	○	○	○	○
Data theft could render my online user accounts unusable.	○	○	○	○	○	○	○
I am afraid that one of my online user	○	○	○	○	○	○	○

data leaks in online user accounts

[]Assessing the relevance and timeliness of data leaks in private user accounts

Please choose the appropriate response for each item.

	Strongly disagree	Disagree	Somewhat disagree	Neither agree nor disagree	Somewhat agree	Agree	Strongly agree
... of my online user accounts.	○	○	○	○	○	○	○
Changing passwords regularly would require too much time.	○	○	○	○	○	○	○
Permanent password changes are a good way to protect my data from data theft on one of my online user accounts.	○	○	○	○	○	○	○
By permanently changing passwords I would reduce the possibility of data theft on one of my online user accounts.	○	○	○	○	○	○	○
I am able to protect my personal user accounts from data theft.	○	○	○	○	○	○	○
Protecting my personal user accounts from data theft is a big effort for me.	○	○	○	○	○	○	○
I feel comfortable taking measures to increase the security of my online user ...	○	○	○	○	○	○	○
The cost of regularly changing the password reduces the convenience of the application.	○	○	○	○	○	○	○
I do not attach great importance to the regular change of my passwords.	○	○	○	○	○	○	○
Potential data leaks are alarming.	○	○	○	○	○	○	○
Data theft could render my online user accounts unusable.	○	○	○	○	○	○	○
I am afraid that one of my online user ...	○	○	○	○	○	○	○

accounts is affected by data theft.							
I will take precautions in the future to protect my online user accounts from data theft.	O	O	O	O	O	O	O
I intend to change my passwords regularly over the next three months.	O	O	O	O	O	O	O
I predict changing my passwords regularly for the next three months.	O	O	O	O	O	O	O

Done - all questions are now answered!

Thank you for your participation

Have you ever been informed that your online user accounts were already involved in a "break" (=data leak)? It would be advisable to use new passwords in the future and to change them regularly. If you have any questions or are interested in this topic, please contact me at

13.06.2018 – 12:45

Submit your survey.
Thank you for completing this survey.

B. Research done so far

Journal	Threat Target	Behavior Context	only PMT used	Results	Fear Appeal	Variables adopted from PMT (core&full)	Variables missing
Anderson and Agarwal, 2010	Home users	Intentions to take safety precautions	no	higher ownership an individual feels for computer, higher protection intentions	no	Protection motivation Response efficacy Self-efficacy	Fear Maladaptive rewards Response costs Threat severity Threat vulnerability
Boss et al., 2015	Students	Intentions and actual data back-up and use of anti-malware	yes	response efficacy, response cost & high treat : significant on intention	yes	Fear Maladaptive rewards Protection motivation Response efficacy Response costs Self-efficacy Threat severity Threat vulnerability	Maladaptive rewards (study 1)
Claar and Johnson, 2012	Students and undefined	Home PC security	no	Severity not sustained	no	Self-efficacy Threat severity Threat vulnerability	Fear Maladaptive rewards Protection motivation Response efficacy Response costs
Crossler, 2010	Employees, students and undefined	Personal computer: Actual adoption of data backup measures	yes	Self-efficacy and response efficacy pos. relationship data back up, threat appraisal constructs negative one	no	Response efficacy Response costs Self-efficacy Threat severity Threat vulnerability	Fear Maladaptive rewards Protection motivation

Study	Sample	Dependent variable		Results		Significant factors	Non-significant / other factors
Crossler and Belanger, 2014	Students	Security behaviors	yes	Response costs were of no significance	no	Response efficacy Response costs Self-efficacy Threat severity Threat vulnerability	Fear Maladaptive rewards Protection motivation
Crossler et al., 2014	Mixed	Organization: Intentions and actual compliance	yes	Vulnerability and response costs: no significance; self-efficacy and response efficacy significance on compliance	no	Protection motivation Response efficacy Response costs Self-efficacy Threat severity Threat vulnerability	Fear Maladaptive rewards
Gurung et al., 2009	Students	Motivations to use anti-spyware	yes	Vulnerability and response costs not supported	no	Response efficacy Self-efficacy Threat severity Threat vulnerability	Protection motivation Response costs Maladaptive rewards Fear
Herath and Rao, 2009	Employees	Intentions to comply with security policies	no	Vulnerability & self-efficacy no significance	no	Protection motivation Response efficacy Response costs Self-efficacy Threat severity Threat vulnerability	Fear Maladaptive rewards
Herath et al., 2012	Students	Intentions to adopt e-mail authentication	no	Privacy concerns found to be reduced with notification practice perceptions	no	Response costs Self-Efficacy	Fear Maladaptive rewards Protection motivation Response efficacy Threat severity Threat vulnerability

Study	Population	Focus		Finding		Constructs	Constructs
Ifinedo, 2012	Employees	Intentions to comply with security policies	no	Perceived security and response cost not significant	no	Protection motivation Response efficacy Response costs Self-efficacy Threat severity Threat vulnerability	Fear Maladaptive rewards
Jenkins et al., 2013	Students	User accounts: Create unique passwords	yes	Fear appeals effective in passwort security	yes	Response efficacy Self efficacy Threat severity Threat vulnerability	Fear Maladaptive rewards Protection motivation Response costs
Johnston and Warkentin, 2010	Employees and students	Personal computer: Intentions to use anti-spyware software	no	Perceived vulnerability not significant	yes	Protection motivation Response efficacy Self-efficacy Threat severity Threat vulnerability	Fear Maladaptive rewards Response costs
Johnston et al., 2015	Employees	Intentions to comply with recommended protective strategies	no	Perceived vulnerability not significant with intentions	yes	Protection motivation Response efficacy Self-efficacy Threat severity Threat vulnerability	Fear Maladaptive rewards Response costs
Lai et al., 2012	Students	Coping with identity theft	no	Coping reduces occurence identitiy theft	no	Protection motivation Self-efficacy	Fear Maladaptive rewards Response efficacy Response costs Threat severity Threat vulnerability
LaRose et al., 2008	Employees	Home computers: Intentions to adopt security measures	no	Self-efficacy significant to intentions	no	Protection motivation Response efficacy Self-efficacy	Fear Maladaptive rewards Response costs

Citation	Population	Dependent variable / behavior		Findings		PMT constructs	Other constructs
							Threat severity; Threat vulnerability
Lee et al., 2008	Students	Intention to use virus-protection	no	Perceived severity not significant on intention	no	Protection motivation; Response efficacy; Self-efficacy; Threat severity; Threat vulnerability	Fear; Maladaptive rewards; Response costs
Lee and Larsen, 2009	Executives	Intentions and actual use of anti-malware software	no	Response efficacy, self-efficacy, and perceived vulnerability no significance on intention	no	Protection motivation; Response efficacy; Response costs; Threat severity; Threat vulnerability	Fear; Maladaptive rewards; Self-efficacy
Lee, 2011	Faculty	Adoption of antiplagiarism software	no	Response cost and self-efficacy no significance on behavior	no	Protection motivation; Response efficacy; Response costs; Self-efficacy; Threat severity; Threat vulnerability	Fear; Maladaptive rewards
Liang and Xue, 2010	Students	Intention & use of anti-spyware software	no	perceived threat, self-efficacy influence protection motivation, perceived threat as mediator	no	Fear; Protection motivation; Response efficacy; Response costs; Self-efficacy; Threat severity; Threat vulnerability	Maladaptive rewards
Marett et al., 2011	Students	Intentions to change risky social media behavior	yes	Extrinsic rewards unexpected positive influence on the	yes	Protection Motivation; Response efficacy; Response costs	Fear; Maladaptive rewards; Threat vulnerability

				threat appraisal model		Self-efficacy Threat severity	Maladaptive rewards
Mwagwabi, 2018	Mixed	Intentions and behavior: password compliance	yes	Fear appeals raise intentions and behaviour	yes	Fear Protection motivation Response efficacy Response costs Self-efficacy Threat severity Threat vulnerability	Maladaptive rewards
Ng et al., 2009	Employees	E-mail behavior	no	Perceived severity no significance on behavior	no	Self-efficacy Threat severity	Fear Maladaptive rewards Protection motivation Response efficacy Threat vulnerability
Posey et al., 2015	Employees	Intentions and behavior: organization's information assets	no	Fear no significance on behavior	yes	Fear Maladaptive rewards Protection motivation Response efficacy Response costs Self-efficacy Threat severity Threat vulnerability	none
Siponen et al., 2010	Employees	Intentions and actual compliance with information security policies	no	Response efficacy no significance on intention	no	Protection motivation Response efficacy Self-efficacy	Fear Maladaptive rewards Response costs Threat severity Threat vulnerability
	Employees		no		no		

Study	Sample	Dependent variable		Threat appraisal significance on intention		Constructs	Not significant
Siponen et al., 2014		Intentions and actual compliance with information security policies				Maladaptive rewards Protection motivation Response efficacy Self-efficacy Threat severity Threat vulnerability	Fear Response costs
Vance et al., 2013	N.A.	Online accounts: password strength	yes	Fear appeal: Stronger passwords	yes	Fear Protection motivation Response costs Response efficacy Self-efficacy Threat severity Threat vulnerability	Maladaptive rewards
Woon et al., 2005	Students	Adoption of wireless security measures	yes	Self efficacy, response efficacy, response costs, and perceived severity significant on behavior	no	Protection motivation Response efficacy Response costs Self-efficacy Threat severity Threat vulnerability	Fear Maladaptive rewards
Workman et al., 2008	Employees	Compliance with security recommendations	yes	Severity significant on motivation	no	Self-efficacy Threat severity Threat vulnerability	Fear Maladaptive rewards Protection motivation
Zhang and McDowell, 2009	Students	Intentions to use strong password	yes	Neither severity nor vulnerability significance	no	Maladaptive rewards Protection motivation Response efficacy Response costs Threat severity Threat vulnerability	Fear Self-efficacy

Yoon et al, 2012	Students	Security behaviors	no	Response-efficacy and self-efficacy significant students' intention and behavior	no	Protection Motivation Response efficacy Response costs Self-efficacy Threat severity Threat vulnerability	Fear Maladaptive rewards

C. Overview Demographic Data of Participants

Age		Fre-quency	Percen-tage	Valid per-centages	Cumulated percenta-ges
Valid	15	1	,4	,4	,4
	16	1	,4	,4	,8
	17	1	,4	,4	1,1
	19	2	,7	,8	1,9
	20	13	4,6	4,9	6,8
	21	18	6,3	6,8	13,6
	22	10	3,5	3,8	17,4
	23	34	12,0	12,8	30,2
	24	33	11,6	12,5	42,6
	25	48	16,9	18,1	60,8
	26	38	13,4	14,3	75,1
	27	13	4,6	4,9	80,0
	28	15	5,3	5,7	85,7
	29	10	3,5	3,8	89,4
	30	6	2,1	2,3	91,7
	31	4	1,4	1,5	93,2
	32	1	,4	,4	93,6
	33	1	,4	,4	94,0
	34	3	1,1	1,1	95,1
	36	1	,4	,4	95,5
	37	1	,4	,4	95,8
	38	1	,4	,4	96,2
	39	2	,7	,8	97,0
	45	2	,7	,8	97,7
	52	1	,4	,4	98,1
	54	1	,4	,4	98,5
	55	3	1,1	1,1	99,6
	58	1	,4	,4	100,0
	Total	265	93,3	100,0	
Missing	System	19	6,7		
Total		284	100,0		

Nationality

		Fre-quency	Percen-tage	Valid per-centages	Cumulated percenta-ges
Valid		19	6,7	6,7	6,7
	Asian	1	,4	,4	7,0
	Australian	1	,4	,4	7,4
	Austrian	9	3,2	3,2	10,6
	Brasilian	1	,4	,4	10,9
	British	7	2,5	2,5	13,4
	Bulgarian	4	1,4	1,4	14,8
	Canadian	1	,4	,4	15,1
	Chinese	3	1,1	1,1	16,2
	Columbian	1	,4	,4	16,5
	Croatian	1	,4	,4	16,9
	Czech	1	,4	,4	17,3
	Dutch	12	4,2	4,2	21,5
	Ecuadorian	1	,4	,4	21,8
	French	3	1,1	1,1	22,9
	German	194	68,3	68,3	91,2
	German/British	1	,4	,4	91,5
	Irish	1	,4	,4	91,9
	Israeli	3	1,1	1,1	93,0
	Italian	2	,7	,7	93,7
	Lithuanian	1	,4	,4	94,0
	Mexican	1	,4	,4	94,4
	Nepali	1	,4	,4	94,7
	Polish	2	,7	,7	95,4
	Republic of Kore	1	,4	,4	95,8
	Romanian	3	1,1	1,1	96,8
	Russian	1	,4	,4	97,2
	Scottish	1	,4	,4	97,5
	Singaporean	1	,4	,4	97,9
	South African	1	,4	,4	98,2
	Spanish	1	,4	,4	98,6
	Swiss	1	,4	,4	98,9

Taiwanese	2	,7	,7	99,6
USA	1	,4	,4	100,0
Total	284	100,0	100,0	

Gender

		Fre-quency	Per-cen-tage	Valid per-centa-ges	Cumu-lated percen-tages
Valid	fe-male	169	59,5	63,8	63,8
	male	96	33,8	36,2	100,0
	total	265	93,3	100,0	
Missing	Sys-tem	19	6,7		
Total		284	100,0		

Current professio-nal status

	t	Fre-quency	Percen-tage	Valid per-centages	Cumulated percenta-ges
Gültig		18	6,3	6,3	6,3
	Pupil	3	1,1	1,1	7,4
	Student	197	69,4	69,4	76,8
	Apprentice/r	3	1,1	1,1	77,8
	Employee	49	17,3	17,3	95,1
	Self-employed	8	2,8	2,8	97,9
	Other	6	2,1	2,1	100,0
	Gesamt	284	100,0	100,0	

D. Multiple Linear Regression

D.1   Regression for Protection Motivation – with Data Leak

REGRESSION

/DESCRIPTIVES MEAN STDDEV CORR SIG N

/SELECT=T001 EQ 'A1'

/MISSING LISTWISE

/STATISTICS COEFF OUTS CI(95) R ANOVA COLLIN TOL ZPP

/CRITERIA=PIN(.05) POUT(.10)

/NOORIGIN

/DEPENDENT prot_moti

/METHOD=ENTER fear res_cost self_effi res_effi mala_rew p_threats vulnerb

/PARTIALPLOT ALL

/RESIDUALS DURBIN HISTOGRAM(ZRESID) NORMPROB(ZRESID)

/CASEWISE PLOT(ZRESID) OUTLIERS(3).

Descriptive Statistics[a]

	Mean	Std. Deviation	N
prot_moti	3,4291	1,56624	94
fear	2,7660	1,05842	94
res_cost	3,3582	1,22912	94
self_effi	3,4574	,79271	94
res_effi	2,6099	1,37188	94
mala_rew	3,2500	1,13362	94
p_threats	2,6879	1,04705	94
vulnerb	3,0709	,71320	94

a. Selecting only cases for which Liegt laut der Website ein Datenleck bei einem deiner Online-Nutzerkonten vor? = A1

Correlations[a]

		prot_moti	fear	res_cost	self_effi	res_effi
Pearson Correlation	prot_moti	1,000	,522	-,079	,278	,356
	fear	,522	1,000	,151	,501	,437
	res_cost	-,079	,151	1,000	,097	,239
	self_effi	,278	,501	,097	1,000	,292
	res_effi	,356	,437	,239	,292	1,000
	mala_rew	,074	,272	,675	,143	,379
	p_threats	,241	,550	,299	,257	,295
	vulnerb	,161	,350	,202	,248	,202
Sig. (1-tailed)	prot_moti	.	,000	,225	,003	,000
	fear	,000	.	,074	,000	,000
	res_cost	,225	,074	.	,175	,010
	self_effi	,003	,000	,175	.	,002
	res_effi	,000	,000	,010	,002	.
	mala_rew	,239	,004	,000	,085	,000
	p_threats	,010	,000	,002	,006	,002
	vulnerb	,061	,000	,025	,008	,025
N	prot_moti	94	94	94	94	94
	fear	94	94	94	94	94
	res_cost	94	94	94	94	94
	self_effi	94	94	94	94	94
	res_effi	94	94	94	94	94
	mala_rew	94	94	94	94	94
	p_threats	94	94	94	94	94
	vulnerb	94	94	94	94	94

Correlations^a

		mala_rew	p_threats	vulnerb
Pearson Correlation	prot_moti	,074	,241	,161
	fear	,272	,550	,350
	res_cost	,675	,299	,202
	self_effi	,143	,257	,248
	res_effi	,379	,295	,202
	mala_rew	1,000	,362	,284
	p_threats	,362	1,000	,436
	vulnerb	,284	,436	1,000
Sig. (1-tailed)	prot_moti	,239	,010	,061
	fear	,004	,000	,000
	res_cost	,000	,002	,025
	self_effi	,085	,006	,008
	res_effi	,000	,002	,025
	mala_rew	.	,000	,003
	p_threats	,000	.	,000
	vulnerb	,003	,000	.
N	prot_moti	94	94	94
	fear	94	94	94
	res_cost	94	94	94
	self_effi	94	94	94
	res_effi	94	94	94
	mala_rew	94	94	94
	p_threats	94	94	94
	vulnerb	94	94	94

a. Selecting only cases for which Liegt laut der Website ein Datenleck bei einem deiner Online-Nutzerkonten vor? = A1

a. Dependent Variable: prot_moti

b. Models are based only on cases for which Liegt laut der Website ein Datenleck bei einem deiner Online-Nutzerkonten vor? = A1

c. All requested variables entered.

Model Summary[b,c]

Model	R Liegt laut der Website ein Datenleck bei einem deiner Online-Nutzerkonten vor? = A1 (Selected)	Liegt laut der Website ein Datenleck bei einem deiner Online-Nutzerkonten vor? ~= A1 (Unselected)	R Square	Adjusted R Square	Std. Error of the Estimate
1	,574[a]	,599	,330	,275	1,33335

Model Summary[b,c]

	Durbin-Watson Statistic	
Model	Liegt laut der Website ein Datenleck bei einem deiner Online-Nutzerkonten vor? = A1 (Selected)	Liegt laut der Website ein Datenleck bei einem deiner Online-Nutzerkonten vor? ~= A1 (Unselected)
1	1,575	1,422

a. Predictors: (Constant), vulnerb, res_effi, res_cost, self_effi, p_threats, fear, mala_rew

b. Unless noted otherwise, statistics are based only on cases for which Liegt laut der Website ein Datenleck bei einem deiner Online-Nutzerkonten vor? = A1.

c. Dependent Variable: prot_moti

ANOVA^{a,b}

Model		Sum of Squares	df	Mean Square	F	Sig.
1	Regression	75,245	7	10,749	6,046	,000^c
	Residual	152,893	86	1,778		
	Total	228,138	93			

a. Dependent Variable: prot_moti

b. Selecting only cases for which Liegt laut der Website ein Datenleck bei einem deiner Online-Nutzerkonten vor? = A1

c. Predictors: (Constant), vulnerb, res_effi, res_cost, self_effi, p_threats, fear, mala_rew

Coefficients^{a,b}

Model		Unstandardized Coefficients		Standardized Coefficients	t	Sig.
		B	Std. Error	Beta		
1	(Constant)	1,742	,814		2,141	,035
	fear	,698	,183	,472	3,815	,000
	res_cost	-,254	,154	-,200	-1,656	,101
	self_effi	,015	,204	,008	,075	,940
	res_effi	,225	,118	,197	1,903	,060
	mala_rew	,018	,177	,013	,104	,917
	p_threats	-,036	,172	-,024	-,209	,835
	vulnerb	,002	,221	,001	,010	,992

Coefficients^{a,b}

Model		95,0% Confidence Interval for B		Correlations		
		Lower Bound	Upper Bound	Zero-order	Partial	Part
1	(Constant)	,124	3,360			
	fear	,334	1,062	,522	,380	,337
	res_cost	-,560	,051	-,079	-,176	-,146
	self_effi	-,390	,420	,278	,008	,007

res_effi	-,010	,459	,356	,201	,168
mala_rew	-,334	,371	,074	,011	,009
p_threats	-,377	,306	,241	-,023	-,018
vulnerb	-,437	,442	,161	,001	,001

Coefficients[a,b]

Model		Collinearity Statistics	
		Tolerance	VIF
1	(Constant)		
	fear	,509	1,964
	res_cost	,536	1,867
	self_effi	,733	1,364
	res_effi	,729	1,372
	mala_rew	,473	2,113
	p_threats	,591	1,692
	vulnerb	,769	1,301

a. Dependent Variable: prot_moti

b. Selecting only cases for which Liegt laut der Website ein Datenleck bei einem deiner Online-Nutzerkonten vor? = A1

Collinearity Diagnostics[a,b]

Model	Dimension	Eigenvalue	Condition Index	Variance Proportions			
				(Constant)	fear	res_cost	self_effi
1	1	7,480	1,000	,00	,00	,00	,00
	2	,160	6,832	,01	,01	,04	,00
	3	,134	7,466	,00	,10	,14	,02
	4	,087	9,263	,06	,03	,01	,08
	5	,054	11,814	,02	,57	,05	,02
	6	,036	14,395	,00	,03	,51	,08
	7	,030	15,861	,01	,17	,23	,30

8	,019	20,006	,90	,09	,01	,51

Collinearity Diagnostics[a,b]

Variance Proportions

Model	Dimension	res_effi	mala_rew	p_threats	vulnerb
1	1	,00	,00	,00	,00
	2	,73	,01	,00	,01
	3	,09	,08	,05	,01
	4	,02	,01	,44	,02
	5	,12	,02	,26	,12
	6	,03	,62	,08	,13
	7	,01	,25	,16	,45
	8	,00	,00	,00	,25

a. Dependent Variable: prot_moti

b. Selecting only cases for which Liegt laut der Website ein Datenleck bei einem deiner Online-Nutzerkonten vor? = A1

Residuals Statistics[a,b]

Liegt laut der Website ein Datenleck bei einem deiner Online-Nutzerkonten vor? = A1 (Selected)

	Minimum	Maximum	Mean	Std. Deviation
Predicted Value	1,6883	5,8532	3,4291	,89949
Residual	-2,20255	3,31172	,00000	1,28219
Std. Predicted Value	-1,935	2,695	,000	1,000
Std. Residual	-1,652	2,484	,000	,962

Residuals Statistics[a,b]

	Liegt laut der Website ein Datenleck bei einem deiner Online-Nutzerkonten vor? = A1 (Selected)	Liegt laut der Website ein Datenleck bei einem deiner Online-Nutzerkonten vor? ~= A1 (Unselected)		
	N	Minimum	Maximum	Mean
Predicted Value	94	1,3577	6,6440	3,6535
Residual	94	-3,08313	2,87603	,48269
Std. Predicted Value	94	-2,303	3,574	,250
Std. Residual	94	-2,312	2,157	,362

Residuals Statistics[a,b]

	Liegt laut der Website ein Datenleck bei einem deiner Online-Nutzerkonten vor? ~= A1 (Unselected)	
	Std. Deviation	N
Predicted Value	,90589	115
Residual	1,10270	115
Std. Predicted Value	1,007	115
Std. Residual	,827	115

a. Dependent Variable: prot_moti

b. Pooled Cases

Charts

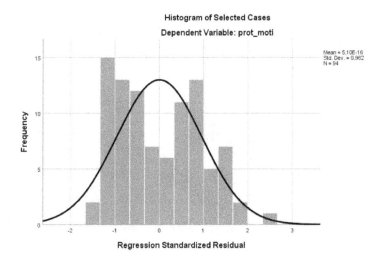

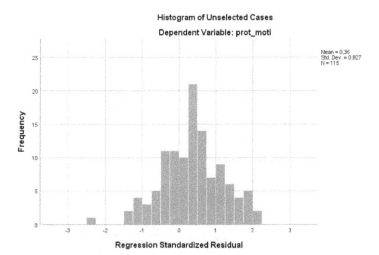

Normal P-P Plot of Standardized Residual for Selected Cases

Dependent Variable: prot_moti

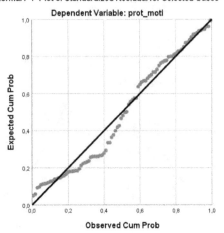

Normal P-P Plot of Standardized Residual for Unselected Cases

Dependent Variable: prot_moti

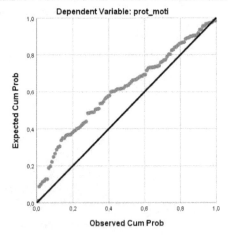

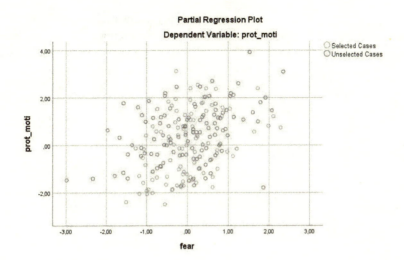

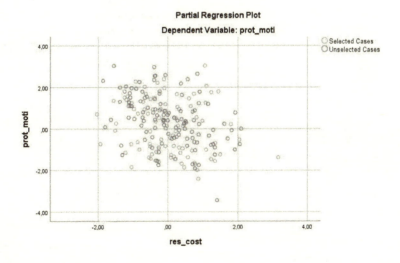

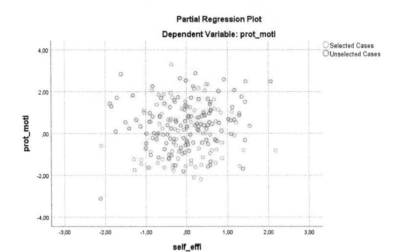

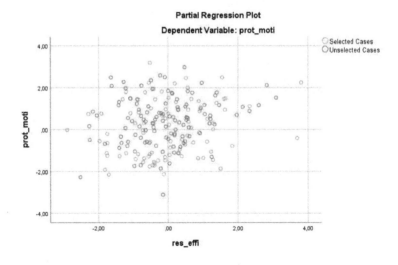

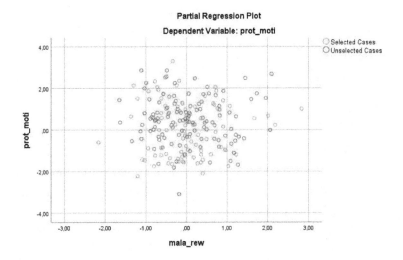

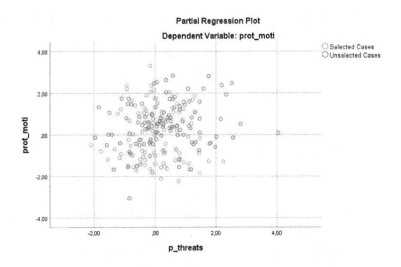

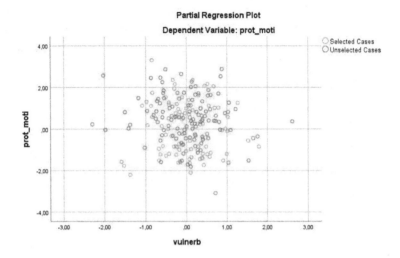

Partial Regression Plot

Dependent Variable: prot_moti

D.2   Regression for Protection Motivation – without Data Leak

REGRESSION

/DESCRIPTIVES MEAN STDDEV CORR SIG N

/SELECT=T001 EQ 'A2'

/MISSING LISTWISE

/STATISTICS COEFF OUTS CI(95) R ANOVA COLLIN TOL ZPP

/CRITERIA=PIN(.05) POUT(.10)

/NOORIGIN

/DEPENDENT prot_moti

/METHOD=ENTER fear res_cost self_effi res_effi mala_rew p_threats vulnerb

/PARTIALPLOT ALL

/RESIDUALS DURBIN HISTOGRAM(ZRESID) NORMPROB(ZRESID)

/CASEWISE PLOT(ZRESID) OUTLIERS(3).

Descriptive Statistics[a]

	Mean	Std. Deviation	N
prot_moti	4,1362	1,37288	115
fear	3,1580	1,05475	115
res_cost	3,6551	1,26578	115
self_effi	3,5797	,84936	115
res_effi	2,7942	1,19092	115
mala_rew	3,5717	1,21204	115
p_threats	3,3406	1,22363	115
vulnerb	3,2870	,90147	115

Correlations[a]

		prot_moti	fear	res_cost	self_effi	res_effi
Pearson Correlation	prot_moti	1,000	,456	-,458	,179	,267
	fear	,456	1,000	,057	,247	,423
	res_cost	-,458	,057	1,000	,228	,092
	self_effi	,179	,247	,228	1,000	,299
	res_effi	,267	,423	,092	,299	1,000
	mala_rew	-,247	,159	,715	,310	,248
	p_threats	,206	,402	,072	,251	,136
	vulnerb	,006	,312	,299	,191	,257
Sig. (1-tailed)	prot_moti	.	,000	,000	,028	,002
	fear	,000	.	,273	,004	,000
	res_cost	,000	,273	.	,007	,165
	self_effi	,028	,004	,007	.	,001
	res_effi	,002	,000	,165	,001	.
	mala_rew	,004	,045	,000	,000	,004
	p_threats	,014	,000	,221	,003	,073
	vulnerb	,475	,000	,001	,021	,003
N	prot_moti	115	115	115	115	115
	fear	115	115	115	115	115

res_cost	115	115	115	115	115
self_effi	115	115	115	115	115
res_effi	115	115	115	115	115
mala_rew	115	115	115	115	115
p_threats	115	115	115	115	115
vulnerb	115	115	115	115	115

Correlations[a]

		mala_rew	p_threats	vulnerb
Pearson Correlation	prot_moti	-,247	,206	,006
	fear	,159	,402	,312
	res_cost	,715	,072	,299
	self_effi	,310	,251	,191
	res_effi	,248	,136	,257
	mala_rew	1,000	,178	,393
	p_threats	,178	1,000	,520
	vulnerb	,393	,520	1,000
Sig. (1-tailed)	prot_moti	,004	,014	,475
	fear	,045	,000	,000
	res_cost	,000	,221	,001
	self_effi	,000	,003	,021
	res_effi	,004	,073	,003
	mala_rew	.	,029	,000
	p_threats	,029	.	,000
	vulnerb	,000	,000	.
N	prot_moti	115	115	115
	fear	115	115	115
	res_cost	115	115	115
	self_effi	115	115	115
	res_effi	115	115	115
	mala_rew	115	115	115

	p_threats	115	115	115
	vulnerb	115	115	115

Model Summary^{b,c}

Model	R Liegt laut der Website ein Datenleck bei einem deiner Online-Nutzer- konten vor? = A2 (Selected)	Liegt laut der Website ein Datenleck bei einem deiner Online-Nutzer- konten vor? ~= A2 (Unsel- ected)	R Square	Adjusted R Square	Std. Error of the Estimate
1	,696ª	,494	,484	,451	1,01757

Model Summary^{b,c}

	Durbin-Watson Statistic	
Model	Liegt laut der Website ein Datenleck bei einem deiner Online-Nutzerkonten vor? = A2 (Selected)	Liegt laut der Website ein Datenleck bei einem deiner Online-Nutzerkonten vor? ~= A2 (Unselected)
1	1,779	1,226

a. Predictors: (Constant), vulnerb, self_effi, res_cost, res_effi, fear, p_threats, mala_rew

b. Unless noted otherwise, statistics are based only on cases for which Liegt laut der Website ein Datenleck bei einem deiner Online-Nutzerkonten vor? = A2.

c. Dependent Variable: prot_moti

ANOVA^{a,b}

Model		Sum of Squares	df	Mean Square	F	Sig.
1	Regression	104,072	7	14,867	14,358	,000ᶜ

Residual	110,794	107	1,035		
Total	214,866	114			

a. Dependent Variable: prot_moti

b. Selecting only cases for which Liegt laut der Website ein Datenleck bei einem deiner Online-Nutzerkonten vor? = A2

c. Predictors: (Constant), vulnerb, self_effi, res_cost, res_effi, fear, p_threats, mala_rew

Coefficients[a,b]

Model		Unstandardized Coefficients		Standardized Coefficients	t	Sig.
		B	Std. Error	Beta		
1	(Constant)	3,316	,528		6,284	,000
	fear	,512	,108	,394	4,729	,000
	res_cost	-,549	,110	-,506	-5,005	,000
	self_effi	,268	,125	,166	2,148	,034
	res_effi	,122	,094	,106	1,300	,196
	mala_rew	-,019	,121	-,017	-,156	,876
	p_threats	,063	,098	,056	,638	,525
	vulnerb	-,071	,135	-,047	-,524	,601

Coefficients[a,b]

Model		95,0% Confidence Interval for B		Correlations		
		Lower Bound	Upper Bound	Zero-order	Partial	Part
1	(Constant)	2,270	4,362			
	fear	,298	,727	,456	,416	,328
	res_cost	-,766	-,331	-,458	-,436	-,347
	self_effi	,021	,515	,179	,203	,149
	res_effi	-,064	,307	,267	,125	,090
	mala_rew	-,258	,220	-,247	-,015	-,011
	p_threats	-,132	,257	,206	,062	,044

vulnerb	-,339	,197	,006	-,051	-,036

Coefficients[a,b]

Model		Collinearity Statistics	
		Tolerance	VIF
1	(Constant)		
	fear	,696	1,438
	res_cost	,472	2,121
	self_effi	,809	1,236
	res_effi	,731	1,369
	mala_rew	,424	2,358
	p_threats	,629	1,589
	vulnerb	,611	1,638

a. Dependent Variable: prot_moti

b. Selecting only cases for which Liegt laut der Website ein Datenleck bei einem deiner Online-Nutzerkonten vor? = A2

Collinearity Diagnostics[a,b]

Model	Dimension	Eigenvalue	Condition Index	Variance Proportions			
				(Constant)	fear	res_cost	self_effi
1	1	7,523	1,000	,00	,00	,00	,00
	2	,153	7,023	,00	,07	,12	,00
	3	,122	7,840	,00	,00	,01	,00
	4	,059	11,248	,09	,12	,00	,22
	5	,054	11,759	,04	,77	,04	,16
	6	,039	13,964	,09	,00	,00	,10
	7	,028	16,289	,03	,01	,70	,07
	8	,021	18,718	,74	,02	,13	,45

Collinearity Diagnostics^{a,b}

Model	Dimension	Variance Proportions res_effi	mala_rew	p_threats	vulnerb
1	1	,00	,00	,00	,00
	2	,16	,06	,03	,00
	3	,44	,01	,25	,02
	4	,21	,04	,18	,07
	5	,07	,02	,02	,01
	6	,01	,07	,38	,59
	7	,10	,62	,10	,07
	8	,01	,17	,04	,24

a. Dependent Variable: prot_moti

b. Selecting only cases for which Liegt laut der Website ein Datenleck bei einem deiner Online-Nutzerkonten vor? = A2

Casewise Diagnostics^a

Case Number	Status	Std. Residual	prot_moti	Predicted Value	Residual
1	X^b	-3,205	1,00	4,2612	-3,26122

a. Dependent Variable: prot_moti

b. Liegt laut der Website ein Datenleck bei einem deiner Online-Nutzerkonten vor? ~= A2 (Unselected)

Residuals Statistics^{a,b}

Liegt laut der Website ein Datenleck bei einem deiner Online-Nutzerkonten vor? = A2 (Selected)

	Minimum	Maximum	Mean	Std. Deviation
Predicted Value	1,8857	6,7588	4,1362	,95546

Residual	-2,76265	2,69221	,00000	,98584
Std. Predicted Value	-2,355	2,745	,000	1,000
Std. Residual	-2,715	2,646	,000	,969

Residuals Statistics[a,b]

	Liegt laut der Website ein Datenleck bei einem deiner Online-Nutzerkonten vor? = A2 (Selected)	Liegt laut der Website ein Datenleck bei einem deiner Online-Nutzerkonten vor? ~= A2 (Unselected)		
	N	Minimum	Maximum	Mean
Predicted Value	115	1,7593	6,5077	4,0236
Residual	115	-3,26122	2,70496	-,59453
Std. Predicted Value	115	-2,488	2,482	-,118
Std. Residual	115	-3,205	2,658	-,584

Residuals Statistics[a,b]

	Liegt laut der Website ein Datenleck bei einem deiner Online-Nutzerkonten vor? ~= A2 (Unselected)	
	Std. Deviation	N
Predicted Value	,93318	94
Residual	1,37097	94
Std. Predicted Value	,977	94
Std. Residual	1,347	94

a. Dependent Variable: prot_moti

b. Pooled Cases

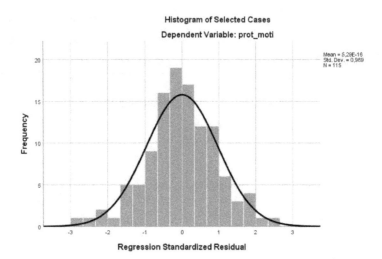

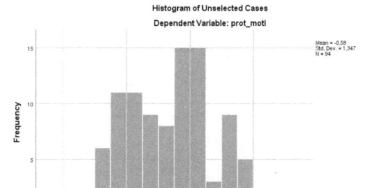

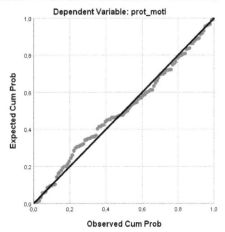

Normal P-P Plot of Standardized Residual for Selected Cases
Dependent Variable: prot_moti

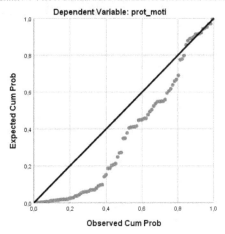

Normal P-P Plot of Standardized Residual for Unselected Cases
Dependent Variable: prot_moti

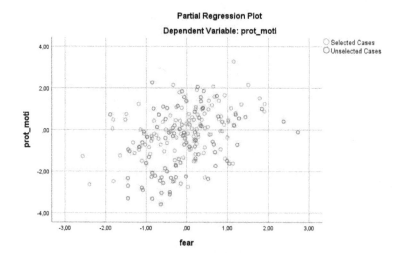

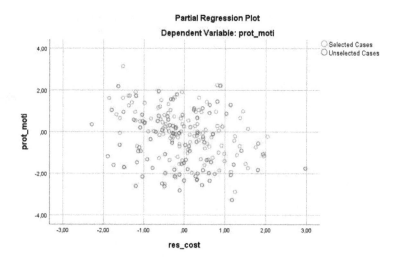

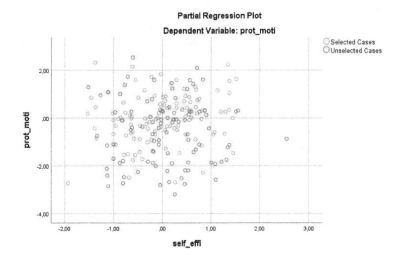

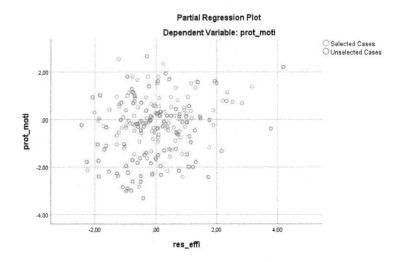

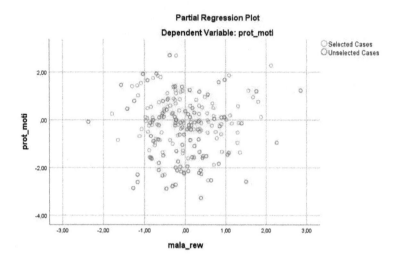

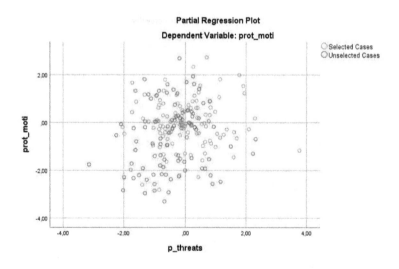

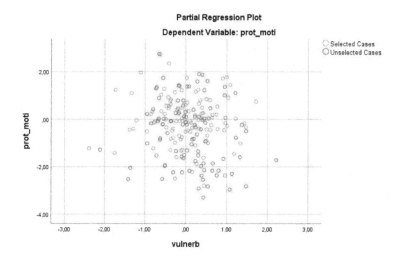

Partial Regression Plot

Dependent Variable: prot_moti

D.3   Regression for Fear – with Data Leak

*

REGRESSION

/DESCRIPTIVES MEAN STDDEV CORR SIG N

/SELECT=T001 EQ 'A1'

/MISSING LISTWISE

/STATISTICS COEFF OUTS CI(95) R ANOVA COLLIN TOL ZPP

/CRITERIA=PIN(.05) POUT(.10)

/NOORIGIN

/DEPENDENT fear

/METHOD=ENTER p_threats vulnerb

/PARTIALPLOT ALL

/RESIDUALS DURBIN HISTOGRAM(ZRESID) NORMPROB(ZRESID)

/CASEWISE PLOT(ZRESID) OUTLIERS(3).

Descriptive Statistics^a

	Mean	Std. Deviation	N
fear	2,7660	1,05842	94
p_threats	2,6879	1,04705	94
vulnerb	3,0709	,71320	94

a. Selecting only cases for which Liegt laut der Website ein Datenleck bei einem deiner Online-Nutzerkonten vor? = A1

Correlations^a

		fear	p_threats	vulnerb
Pearson Correlation	fear	1,000	,550	,350
	p_threats	,550	1,000	,436
	vulnerb	,350	,436	1,000
Sig. (1-tailed)	fear	.	,000	,000
	p_threats	,000	.	,000
	vulnerb	,000	,000	.
N	fear	94	94	94
	p_threats	94	94	94
	vulnerb	94	94	94

a. Selecting only cases for which Liegt laut der Website ein Datenleck bei einem deiner Online-Nutzerkonten vor? = A1

Variables Entered/Removed^{a,b}

Model	Variables Entered	Variables Removed	Method
1	vulnerb, p_threats^c	.	Enter

a. Dependent Variable: fear

b. Models are based only on cases for which Liegt laut der Website ein Datenleck bei einem deiner Online-Nutzerkonten vor? = A1

c. All requested variables entered.

Model Summary^(b,c)

	R				
Model	Liegt laut der Website ein Datenleck bei einem deiner Online-Nutzerkonten vor? = A1 (Selected)	Liegt laut der Website ein Datenleck bei einem deiner Online-Nutzerkonten vor? ~= A1 (Unselected)	R Square	Adjusted R Square	Std. Error of the Estimate
1	,563^a	,418	,317	,302	,88399

Model Summary^(b,c)

	Durbin-Watson Statistic	
Model	Liegt laut der Website ein Datenleck bei einem deiner Online-Nutzerkonten vor? = A1 (Selected)	Liegt laut der Website ein Datenleck bei einem deiner Online-Nutzerkonten vor? ~= A1 (Unselected)
1	1,506	2,332

a. Predictors: (Constant), vulnerb, p_threats

b. Unless noted otherwise, statistics are based only on cases for which Liegt laut der Website ein Datenleck bei einem deiner Online-Nutzerkonten vor? = A1.

c. Dependent Variable: fear

ANOVA[a,b]

Model		Sum of Squares	df	Mean Square	F	Sig.
1	Regression	33,074	2	16,537	21,162	,000[c]
	Residual	71,111	91	,781		
	Total	104,184	93			

a. Dependent Variable: fear

b. Selecting only cases for which Liegt laut der Website ein Datenleck bei einem deiner Online-Nutzerkonten vor? = A1

c. Predictors: (Constant), vulnerb, p_threats

Coefficients[a,b]

Model		Unstandardized Coefficients		Standardized Coefficients	t	Sig.
		B	Std. Error	Beta		
1	(Constant)	,814	,411		1,980	,051
	p_threats	,496	,097	,491	5,100	,000
	vulnerb	,201	,143	,136	1,410	,162

Coefficients[a,b]

Model		95,0% Confidence Interval for B		Correlations		
		Lower Bound	Upper Bound	Zero-order	Partial	Part
1	(Constant)	-,003	1,631			
	p_threats	,303	,689	,550	,471	,442
	vulnerb	-,082	,485	,350	,146	,122

Coefficients[a,b]

Model		Collinearity Statistics	
		Tolerance	VIF
1	(Constant)		

p_threats		,810	1,235
vulnerb		,810	1,235

a. Dependent Variable: fear

b. Selecting only cases for which Liegt laut der Website ein Datenleck bei einem deiner Online-Nutzerkonten vor? = A1

Collinearity Diagnostics[a,b]

Model	Dimension	Eigenvalue	Condition Index	Variance Proportions		
				(Constant)	p_threats	vulnerb
1	1	2,901	1,000	,01	,01	,00
	2	,075	6,235	,16	,93	,05
	3	,025	10,829	,83	,05	,94

a. Dependent Variable: fear

b. Selecting only cases for which Liegt laut der Website ein Datenleck bei einem deiner Online-Nutzerkonten vor? = A1

Casewise Diagnostics[a]

Case Number	Status	Std. Residual	fear	Predicted Value	Residual
48	X[b]	-3,580	1,33	4,4981	-3,16478
220	X[b]	3,236	6,00	3,1390	2,86098

a. Dependent Variable: fear

b. Liegt laut der Website ein Datenleck bei einem deiner Online-Nutzerkonten vor? ~= A1 (Unselected)

Residuals Statistics[a,b]

Liegt laut der Website ein Datenleck bei einem deiner Online-
Nutzerkonten vor? = A1 (Selected)

	Minimum	Maximum	Mean	Std. Deviation
Predicted Value	1,7128	4,9631	2,7660	,59635
Residual	-1,93767	2,53019	,00000	,87443
Std. Predicted Value	-1,766	3,684	,000	1,000
Std. Residual	-2,192	2,862	,000	,989

Residuals Statistics[a,b]

	Liegt laut der Website ein Datenleck bei einem deiner Online-Nutzerkonten vor? = A1 (Selected)	Liegt laut der Website ein Datenleck bei einem deiner Online-Nutzerkonten vor? ~= A1 (Unselected)		
	N	Minimum	Maximum	Mean
Predicted Value	94	1,7799	5,6966	3,1333
Residual	94	-3,16478	2,86098	,02469
Std. Predicted Value	94	-1,653	4,914	,616
Std. Residual	94	-3,580	3,236	,028

Residuals Statistics[a,b]

	Liegt laut der Website ein Datenleck bei einem deiner On-line-Nutzerkonten vor? ~= A1 (Unselected)	
	Std. Deviation	N
Predicted Value	,71843	115
Residual	,99745	115
Std. Predicted Value	1,205	115
Std. Residual	1,128	115

a. Dependent Variable: fear

b. Pooled Cases

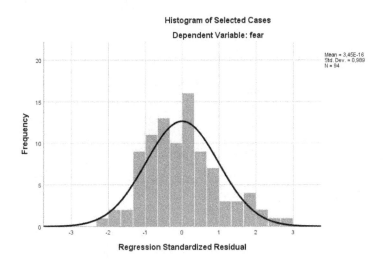

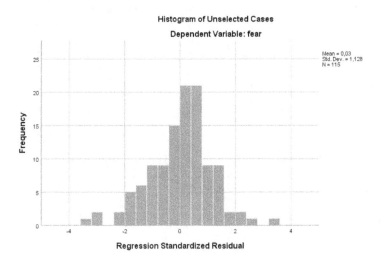

Normal P-P Plot of Standardized Residual for Selected Cases

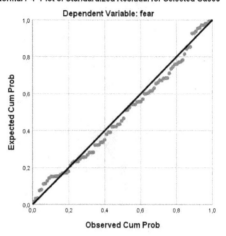

Normal P-P Plot of Standardized Residual for Unselected Cases

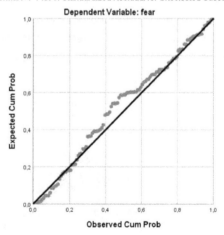

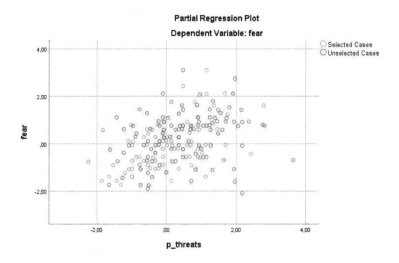

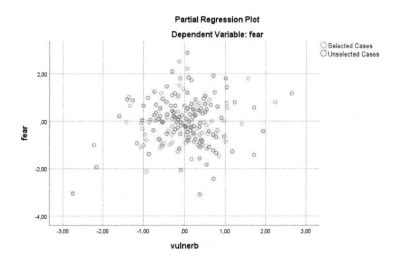

ohne Datenleck

D.4   Regression for Fear – without Data Leak

REGRESSION

 /DESCRIPTIVES MEAN STDDEV CORR SIG N

 /SELECT=T001 EQ 'A2'

 /MISSING LISTWISE

 /STATISTICS COEFF OUTS CI(95) R ANOVA COLLIN TOL ZPP

 /CRITERIA=PIN(.05) POUT(.10)

 /NOORIGIN

 /DEPENDENT fear

 /METHOD=ENTER p_threats vulnerb

 /PARTIALPLOT ALL

 /RESIDUALS DURBIN HISTOGRAM(ZRESID) NORMPROB(ZRESID)

 /CASEWISE PLOT(ZRESID) OUTLIERS(3).

Descriptive Statistics[a]

	Mean	Std. Deviation	N
fear	3,1580	1,05475	115
p_threats	3,3406	1,22363	115
vulnerb	3,2870	,90147	115

a. Selecting only cases for which Liegt laut der Website ein Datenleck bei einem deiner Online-Nutzerkonten vor? = A2

Correlations[a]

		fear	p_threats	vulnerb
Pearson Correlation	fear	1,000	,402	,312
	p_threats	,402	1,000	,520
	vulnerb	,312	,520	1,000
Sig. (1-tailed)	fear	.	,000	,000

	p_threats	,000	.	,000
	vulnerb	,000	,000	.
N	fear	115	115	115
	p_threats	115	115	115
	vulnerb	115	115	115

a. Selecting only cases for which Liegt laut der Website ein Datenleck bei einem deiner Online-Nutzerkonten vor? = A2

Variables Entered/Removed[a,b]

Model	Variables Entered	Variables Removed	Method
1	vulnerb, p_threats[c]	.	Enter

a. Dependent Variable: fear

b. Models are based only on cases for which Liegt laut der Website ein Datenleck bei einem deiner Online-Nutzerkonten vor? = A2

c. All requested variables entered.

Model Summary[b,c]

Model	R Liegt laut der Website ein Datenleck bei einem deiner Online-Nutzerkonten vor? = A2 (Selected)	Liegt laut der Website ein Datenleck bei einem deiner Online-Nutzerkonten vor? ~= A2 (Unselected)	R Square	Adjusted R Square	Std. Error of the Estimate
1	,419[a]	,562	,176	,161	,96606

Model Summary[b,c]

Durbin-Watson Statistic

Model	Liegt laut der Website ein Datenleck bei einem deiner Online-Nutzerkonten vor? = A2 (Selected)	Liegt laut der Website ein Datenleck bei einem deiner Online-Nutzerkonten vor? ~= A2 (Unselected)
1	2,360	1,367

a. Predictors: (Constant), vulnerb, p_threats

b. Unless noted otherwise, statistics are based only on cases for which Liegt laut der Website ein Datenleck bei einem deiner Online-Nutzerkonten vor? = A2.

c. Dependent Variable: fear

ANOVA[a,b]

Model		Sum of Squares	df	Mean Square	F	Sig.
1	Regression	22,297	2	11,149	11,946	,000[c]
	Residual	104,527	112	,933		
	Total	126,825	114			

a. Dependent Variable: fear

b. Selecting only cases for which Liegt laut der Website ein Datenleck bei einem deiner Online-Nutzerkonten vor? = A2

c. Predictors: (Constant), vulnerb, p_threats

Coefficients[a,b]

Model		Unstandardized Coefficients		Standardized Coefficients	t	Sig.
		B	Std. Error	Beta		
1	(Constant)	1,670	,353		4,728	,000
	p_threats	,283	,087	,328	3,269	,001
	vulnerb	,165	,117	,141	1,404	,163

Coefficients^(a,b)

Model		95,0% Confidence Interval for B		Correlations		
		Lower Bound	Upper Bound	Zero-order	Partial	Part
1	(Constant)	,970	2,370			
	p_threats	,111	,454	,402	,295	,280
	vulnerb	-,068	,398	,312	,132	,120

Coefficients^(a,b)

Model		Collinearity Statistics	
		Tolerance	VIF
1	(Constant)		
	p_threats	,730	1,370
	vulnerb	,730	1,370

a. Dependent Variable: fear

b. Selecting only cases for which Liegt laut der Website ein Datenleck bei einem deiner Online-Nutzerkonten vor? = A2

Collinearity Diagnostics^(a,b)

Model	Dimension	Eigenvalue	Condition Index	Variance Proportions		
				(Constant)	p_threats	vulnerb
1	1	2,905	1,000	,01	,01	,01
	2	,062	6,839	,37	,85	,03
	3	,033	9,390	,63	,14	,97

a. Dependent Variable: fear

b. Selecting only cases for which Liegt laut der Website ein Datenleck bei einem deiner Online-Nutzerkonten vor? = A2

Residuals Statistics^{a,b}

Liegt laut der Website ein Datenleck bei einem deiner Online-Nutzerkonten vor? = A2 (Selected)

	Minimum	Maximum	Mean	Std. Deviation
Predicted Value	2,3226	4,8063	3,1580	,44226
Residual	-2,65557	2,83643	,00000	,95755
Std. Predicted Value	-1,889	3,727	,000	1,000
Std. Residual	-2,749	2,936	,000	,991

Residuals Statistics^{a,b}

	Liegt laut der Website ein Datenleck bei einem deiner Online-Nutzerkonten vor? = A2 (Selected)	Liegt laut der Website ein Datenleck bei einem deiner Online-Nutzerkonten vor? ~= A2 (Unselected)		
	N	Minimum	Maximum	Mean
Predicted Value	115	2,2676	4,2876	2,9376
Residual	115	-1,99856	2,64777	-,17167
Std. Predicted Value	115	-2,013	2,554	-,498
Std. Residual	115	-2,069	2,741	-,178

Residuals Statistics^{a,b}

Liegt laut der Website ein Datenleck bei einem deiner Online-Nutzerkonten vor? ~= A2 (Unselected)

	Std. Deviation	N
Predicted Value	,36343	94
Residual	,90564	94
Std. Predicted Value	,822	94
Std. Residual	,937	94

a. Dependent Variable: fear

b. Pooled Cases

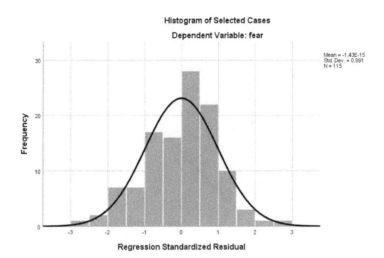

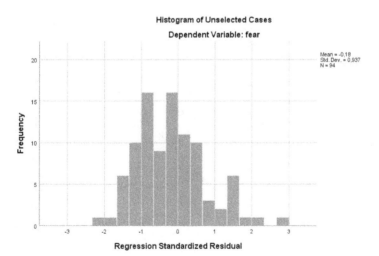

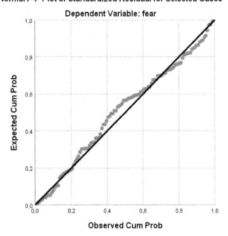

Normal P-P Plot of Standardized Residual for Selected Cases

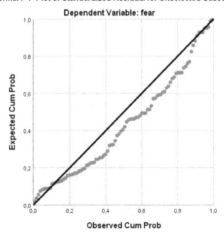

Normal P-P Plot of Standardized Residual for Unselected Cases

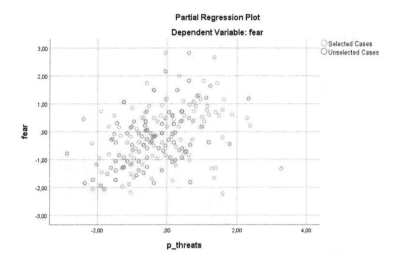

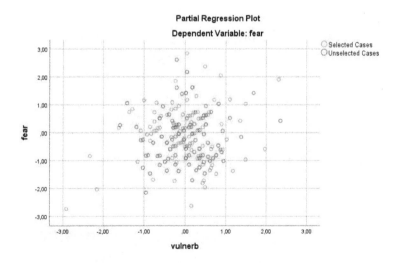